MAN ARISE

MEN'S BIBLE STUDY

Becoming men

who rise up in

spiritual strength

By Skylar Lewis & John Hansen

TABLE OF CONTENTS

THE MAN ARISE BIBLE STUDY
HOW IT WORKS

What does it look like for a man to come into alignment with God's heart for his life? What does it look like for a man to truly be discipled so that his spiritual life reflects the royalty that runs through his veins? What does it look like for a man to live as a beloved son of the King of Kings? This Bible Study will define twelve characteristics and roles of a godly man — and provide the scriptural foundation for a healthy pursuit of God, spiritual formation, discipleship, and transformation so that you will become a man who rises up in spiritual strength!

This Bible study is written for you, designed to illuminate principles that can help you grow as a godly man. You will discover men from the pages of scripture renowned for their godly strength, character, and impact in this world; then, taking cue from their example by gaining a deeper understanding of their lives.

We want you to understand your kingdom assignment! You are invited to be a son, a servant, and a friend in God's Kingdom. Each of us has an assignment to establish and advance God's Kingdom in this world, in and through our lives. At the same time, you are becoming a man of God who recognizes you're called to be a king in this world, not a pawn of this world. This means you need to figure out how to live like a king; not in the worldly sense of the word, but the godly sense of the word. In each chapter, there is a section called 'Your Kingdom Assignment' which will help you understand exactly what it looks like to be a king in this world under the Kingship of your Heavenly Father.

We want you to discuss what you are learning with some other men, because we believe that iron sharpens iron (Proverbs 27:17). The basic discussion questions are helpful, but you'll notice for each number, there will be a question in italics, prefaced with a dash – we call those 'Kings Discussion Questions'. Men who are becoming kings recognize the value of the sharpening that can only occur when we're brutally honest with each other. For that reason, these 'Kings Discussion Questions' are direct; don't shy away from them! Those questions may be the most powerful part of this book, outside of the scriptures themselves. Make sure you do this study with at least two other men, and make sure to hit those questions hard. Leave the most time for those questions, because they will help you grow.

HOW TO USE THIS BIBLE STUDY (MUST READ!)

In each Man Arise chapter, there are six sections. Ideally, you should spend 45 minutes to complete sections 1–4 as pre-work. Then, gather with other men for 45 to 90 minutes to engage in sections 5–6.

Here's a hint: At the very least, you should complete section 4 of the pre-work, so you can engage well in the group session. When you open this book to work on it, have a pen and a highlighter in hand, and mark this book up with underlines, answers, and notes.

DON'T HAVE TIME OR DON'T LIKE TO READ?

We get it. Not everyone has the same appetite for reading or lots of discretionary time. If that's you, you can still do this! Just jump to the sections titled 'Your Kingdom Assignment' and 'Discuss it So You Can Do it', and the 'Kings Discussion Questions' — and just do that!

What's in each chapter — and how to approach the content:

SECTION 1
A CHAPTER READING ABOUT THE TOPIC

Each chapter will start with a brief overview of the topic, with highlights of some of Skylar's or John's personal experience. For section 1, just read the short chapter. It may take you 5–10 minutes. Highlight or underline anything that is meaningful or insightful to you.

SECTION 2
GOD'S MAN: A BIBLE PERSON

We want you to get to know some of the great men of the Bible, so each chapter will introduce you to one. Read the brief description of the Biblical Man of God being highlighted. This will take you 2–3 minutes.

SECTION 3
DIGGING DEEPER

For this section, you will open your Bible and read some portions of scripture. Preferably, open the actual Bible — not just the Bible App! You should read those scripture references, consider the questions, and write down some thoughts and answers. This section will take you 20–30 minutes to complete.

SECTION 4
KINGDOM ASSIGNMENT

Read and underline this section adding any necessary notes. This portion will give you a window into your assignment for and within God's Kingdom with regard to the topic. This should take 5–10 minutes to read.

SECTION 5
KINGS DISCUSSION QUESTIONS

You learn best when you process thoughtful questions in dialogue with others who are focusing on the same topic. We recommend gathering with a small group of men to discuss these questions. You can look up the verses and read them when possible, and consider the bible reference questions and talk about them. For each question, the King's Questions are the true heart of the matter. Feel free to skip right to these if time is short!

SECTION 6
ARISE AND ACCEPT THE CHALLENGE

This section will suggest several ways to actively step into the preferred future God has for you. If you choose to arise and accept the challenge, share it with your group. We recommend committing to these challenges during your group session and discussing the results in the following session.

YOUR FIRST 'ARISE AND ACCEPT THE CHALLENGE'

Going forward, you will find these "Arise and Accept the Challenge" sections at the end of each chapter. However, we want your second Man Arise meeting to start with challenge stories, so we're launching you into this experience with 'Arise and Accept the Challenge' opportunities in order to help you gear up for what's ahead.

1   Tell five people that you are starting a small group study called Man Arise with a group of men to work on spiritual growth in your life. Keep track, and be ready to share the names of who you told.

2   Purchase or dust off your Bible and actually read the Table of Contents. Pick one book of the Bible that appeals to you for any reason, read the first chapter of that book, and highlight one verse you liked.

3   Check your finances and determine how much debt you currently have (personal consumer debt, not home mortgage). List 2–3 worthwhile things that debt represents and be ready to name them.

4   Write down a list of your top five personal strengths and weaknesses. Be ready to share them boldly.

HOW TO LEAD A MAN ARISE GROUP

1 **INVITE A GROUP OF MEN TO GATHER TO GROW!**

Take the initiative to gather a group of men. Man Arise works best in groups of three to eight men. These could be men from work, from the gym, from your kids' school or team, or from the neighborhood. Ask them if they want to be part of a small group with other men who want to grow spiritually. Let them know you'll be using this book, and give them a copy or ask them to buy one online. Find a place that's suitable to gather; this could be a coffee shop, a park, a home, or a restaurant. Agree on a time to meet. Send reminders, and let them know they don't need to do anything at all for this first meeting.

2 **LEAD THE FIRST GATHERING AS AN ORIENTATION**

The first gathering is an orientation — and you're leading it. Have the men introduce themselves and give them the book. Spend time walking them through the ways your group will use the book. Make sure they understand the homework, and issue the first opportunity to 'Arise and Accept the Challenge'. Finally, pray for your brothers and ask God to transform each of you through the study.

Here's a roadmap for this first gathering:

· **Introductions**: Ask each man to introduce himself by sharing his name, family status (married/kids), career, and hobby.

· **Book orientation**: Ask the men to open the book to page 4, and then read the two opening sections aloud: 'How to use this Bible Study' and 'Don't have time...'

· **Ask the men**, "Do you understand this so far? I'm asking you to do about 45 minutes or so of pre-work each week before we meet. Are you in?"

· **Men read sections 1–6 aloud**: Take turns reading through sections 1–6 in the 'What's in this...' segment. Have one man read a segment out loud, and then follow up with a check-in statement like, "Got that?" or "Sound good?" Then proceed to the next section.

- **Ask for commitment**: After reading through pages 4–5, repeat to the guys: "So — guys, I'm asking you to do about 45 minutes of pre-work each week. Can you commit to this?"

- **Arise and Accept the challenge**: Ask the men to turn to page 8 and read through the challenges. Tell them, "Men — these are the challenges. Next week when we meet, we will start by reporting back what we did or didn't do with any of these challenges. So consider taking on one or more!"

- **Give the assignment for the next week**: Tell the guys their assignment for the next week, which is to complete sections 1–4 in chapter 1; do pre-work on sections 5–6 if time permits.

3   HOW TO LEAD EACH GATHERING FOR EACH CHAPTER

Text and call your guys a couple times to remind them about the next gathering. Remind them to do the work. Your text or voice message could say something like this: "Hey man, looking forward to seeing you again for the RUK bible study on Wednesday at Tom's Burgers at 7pm. Just a reminder — this week, work on sections 1–4 — pages 8–13 in the book!" Once you gather with the men, here's a roadmap for leading each weekly meeting:

- **Challenge stories (10 minutes):** Once everyone is settled, food is ordered, etc., ask your guys to turn to the 'Arise and Accept the Challenge' section from the previous week. Ask one guy to just read the 3–5 'challenges' out loud to refresh everyone's memory. Ask each man to take turns and share about one of the 'Arise and Accept' challenges that they did. Ask them to share how they completed the challenge and what they experienced as a result. *At the second Man Arise meeting, you're going to be using the challenge opportunities from page 8 at the beginning of the meeting.

- **Chapter reading highlight (2 minutes):**
  Ask the guys to open to the chapter reading. Ask for one guy to answer this simple question: "What did you get out of the chapter reading overview?" After they share, affirm what they shared.

- **God's Man section (3 minutes):** Tell the guys, "Lets turn to the 'God's man' section of this chapter, and talk briefly about [the highlighted example from scripture].". Pick any one of the questions, and ask one member of the group to answer.

- **Your Kingdom Assignment leader summary (3 minutes):** As the leader, you summarize the 'Kingdom Assignment' section; read the 3–6 main points and sum up what this section is about.

- **Discuss it so you can do it (40 minutes):** Read through the questions in advance. Consider what you know about the men in your group, and then pick the questions you feel led to focus on. Decide ahead of time which questions you want to give more time to and circle those. You may also decide NOT to have guys look up and read every single Bible verse. The Kings Discussion Questions are crucial; direct the group to focus on them.

- **Homework and 'Arise and Accept the Challenge' (3 minutes):** Read the challenges and tell the guys you expect them to do at least one of these challenges. Let them know what you expect them to complete in the book before the next time you meet (i.e., read the next chapter, fully complete sections 1–4, and do pre-work on sections 5–6.)

- **Prayer (3 minutes):** Wrap up the gathering with prayer. Change it up regularly. One week, just ask one man to pray for the whole group. Another week, ask each man to pray for the guy on his right. Another week, you just close in prayer.

A MAN OF FOUR-PILLAR INTENTIONALITY

"Many are the plans in a man's heart, but it is the Lord's purpose that prevails"

Proverbs 19:21 NIV

SKYLAR'S STORY: LEARNING TO BE PRINCIPLED

If you've heard my story, you know that I started the Rise Up Kings movement because of my own experience of living in a way that I knew was beneath my potential. I had some successes in my work life, but I had almost crashed and burned my marriage before it even started because of unfaithfulness and selfishness. It was a dark season for me, and it caused me to do some serious soul-searching about what mattered most and how I could live differently from that point on. I couldn't live life by accident anymore. I decided — 'No more haphazard, careless living! I can do better!' I knew the stories from the Bible about the kings of old who led God's people to victory — and I wanted to follow that example. I wanted to rise up as a king in my own way. To do that, I needed to figure out how to live my life on purpose! During that season of chaos I determined to build my life intentionally on these four pillars: Faith, Family, Fitness, and Finances.

This world is constantly pulling you in different directions, and it would be easy to get caught up in the distractions and temptations of life. Therefore, it is essential for those of us living as kings in God's Kingdom to have strong foundations built on principles and established with intentionality so we can live lives that honor God and make a positive impact on those around us. With that goal in mind, let's discover more about a man of principle in God's Word: Nehemiah.

GOD'S MAN: NEHEMIAH

Nehemiah is a great example of a man who lived with principle, purpose, and intentionality. While we can't create a direct correlation between the four pillars and this one man, we can see a man who would not have been able to have the impact he had if he wasn't strong in his faith, family, fitness, and finances. Nehemiah was a man of deep faith and devotion to God, who lived his life with a clear sense of purpose and direction. One of the most striking examples of Nehemiah's principled disposition can be seen in his response to the news of the broken-down walls of Jerusalem. Despite being in a position of comfort and security as the cupbearer to the king of Persia, Nehemiah was deeply disturbed by the news of the city's distress and immediately sought God's guidance on how he could help. With a clear sense of calling and intentionality, Nehemiah rallied the people of Jerusalem and led them in rebuilding the walls of the city. He faced opposition and setbacks along the way, but he remained steadfast in his commitment to God's purpose for his life. Read the entire book of Nehemiah and discover the principled man of intentionality who rebuilt a city for God's glory.

DIGGING DEEPER: NEHEMIAH

1   **Read Nehemiah 1:1–4** (highly suggest reading all of Nehemiah 1).
    What does Nehemiah's example of prayer and fasting before taking
    action teach us about making decisions in our own lives?

2   **Read Nehemiah 2:17–18** (highly suggest reading all of Nehemiah
    2). What can we learn from Nehemiah's unwavering determination
    and leadership skills as he rallied the people to rebuild the walls of
    Jerusalem?

3   **Read Nehemiah 4:6–14** ((highly suggest reading all of Nehemiah 3–4). How does Nehemiah's response to opposition and criticism reveal a godly approach to handling challenges with courage and perseverance?

4   **Read Nehemiah 5:9–13** (highly suggest reading all of Nehemiah 5). How does Nehemiah's emphasis on personal responsibility challenge you to examine your own life and priorities?

YOUR KINGDOM ASSIGNMENT: BECOME A PRINCIPLED MAN!

The four pillars are the basis around which you can build a principled life. As a man who is rising up in his royal identity and purpose, the four pillars are meant to be the bedrock for your life. Let's explore the biblical foundations of the four pillars.

FAITH

A man's faith is the foundation upon which he builds his life. It is his connection to God and the source of his strength, peace, and hope. Without a strong faith, a man is susceptible to being shaken by life's challenges and temptations. However, when a man trusts in God and seeks His will in all he does, he will find the strength and peace he needs to navigate life's storms. As a Christian man, it is vital that you learn to live with intentionality in your faith by setting aside time for prayer, reading the Bible, and being an active participant in your church.

"Trust in the Lord with all your heart; do not depend on your own understanding. Seek his will in all you do, and he will show you which path to take." (Proverbs 3:5–6 NLT)

FAMILY

Family is a vital part of a man's life and is a gift from God. A man's role as a husband and father is crucial to the health and well-being of his family. When a man leads his family with love and demonstrates his commitment to them through his actions and words, he creates a safe and supportive environment in which the whole family can rise up in their royal identity. Within our Rise Up Kings movement, we regard true friends as part of our extended family. Living with intentionality in your family means setting aside quality time for your wife, children and friends. It means serving and supporting your family and friends, and being present in their lives. Ultimately, this is about you considering the value and honor in the ones God has entrusted to you as family, and cultivating an environment of honor and love where they can thrive, for their good and yours!

"Love each other with genuine affection, and take delight in honoring each other." (Romans 12:10 NLT)

FITNESS

Physical fitness is an essential aspect of a man's overall well-being. When a man takes care of his body, he not only improves his physical health, but also strengthens his mental and emotional well-being. This, in turn, enables him to handle life's challenges and serve others effectively. Living with intentionality in your fitness means setting aside time for exercise, eating a balanced diet, and getting enough sleep. It also means avoiding unhealthy habits and substances, and taking care of your body as a temple of the Holy Spirit.

"Do you not know that your bodies are temples of the Holy Spirit, who is in you, whom you have received from God? You are not your own; you were bought at a price. Therefore honor God with your bodies." (1 Corinthians 6:19–20 NLT)

FINANCE

A man's financial situation has a direct impact on his family, his community, and his future. It is important for you to learn to be a man who is responsible with his finances and manages them in a way that honors God. Rick Warren once said, "Either you will control your money, or your money will control you." Living with intentionality in your finances means creating a budget, saving for the future, and investing in assets that will generate income. It also means avoiding consumer debt, living within your means, and being generous with your resources. More broadly, in the Rise Up Kings community, we consider our finances as something directly connected to our work and our business; after all, our businesses or careers are what allow us to have finances. When we think about finances, we consider how we can lead our businesses more effectively so that we'll have more finances to work with!

"So if you have not been trustworthy in handling worldly wealth, who will trust you with true riches?" (Luke 16:11 NLT)

MAN ARISE AS A MAN OF FOUR PILLAR INTENTIONALITY

I want you to become a man who is principled — who lives with purpose and intentionality in the areas of faith, family, fitness, and finances. Make these the four pillars of your life! If you do, you will experience growth, joy, and peace, and be able to make a positive impact in the world. As a Christian man, it is up to you to prioritize these areas of your life and seek God's will in all you do. By living with intentionality, you will become a principled man; you'll be able to navigate life's challenges with strength and peace, and experience the fullness of life that God has intended for you.

THE REST OF SKYLAR'S STORY

My life has been filled with many valleys, from pornography addiction to selfishness permeating my marriage. It wasn't until I started to lean into Christ and decided to become a Four Pillar Man that I truly transformed. There is hope for men to become all that God has called them to become. Once we accept Christ as our Savior, the work starts. Then we must unwind the character flaws, poor behaviors, and limiting mindsets that we have learned to operate with. We then are able to develop the Godly character that allows us to reach our God-given potential.

KINGS DISCUSSION QUESTIONS

1   Give yourself a quick score (1–10) on each of the four pillars, 10 being the best — just jot the number down for each of the four pillars. Which pillar is going well for you?

Why do you think that pillar is going well?

2   Which of the pillars has the lowest personal 'quick score' on a scale of 1–10?

What's getting in the way of you elevating the score that is currently the lowest?

3   **Read Ephesians 2:8–9, James 2:17, and 2 Corinthians 5:7.** How does your faith impact the way you live your life? What are some practical ways you can deepen your relationship with God?

Share the truth about how you are (or are not) living into — and living out — a strong faith in Christ.

4   **Read Colossians 3:12–13, Ephesians 5:21–27, and Romans 12:10.** What are some basic steps you could be taking to cultivate stronger family relationships?

What is currently your greatest struggle or failure in your family relationships? What is a possible course correction you could start to make right now?

5   **Read 1 Corinthians 6:19–20 and 1 Corinthians 10:31.** How can you use your physical health to glorify God? How is your physical health right now?

What is the best thing you are doing for your body right now? What is one choice or habit are you engaging in that is not supporting your physical health?

6   **Read Matthew 25:14–30 and Proverbs 3:9–10.** What is the role of stewardship in your financial life? How can you manage your finances in a way that honors God?

What is a financial mistake you have made recently? What did you learn from it? Are there any financial patterns in your life right now that you know need to change?

ARISE AND ACCEPT THE CHALLENGE

1   Begin a workout routine for your fitness pillar. We suggest the RUK 300: 100 sit-ups, 100 squats, and 100 pushups daily.

2   Start reading the Bible daily. You can start a one-year Bible plan or use the Bible app.

3   Commit to completing this Man Arise Bible study and tell two other guys about this commitment!

A MAN OF MEANS

"Praise the Lord! How joyful are those who fear the Lord and delight in obeying his commands. Their children will be successful everywhere; an entire generation of godly people will be blessed. They themselves will be wealthy, and their good deeds will last forever."

Psalm 112:1–3

SKYLAR'S STORY:
BECOMING A MAN OF MEANS AND CHANGING MY MINDSET

As a young man, I lived with a lot of ambition. I had a sense that I could take on the world and make great things happen. Because of that inner drive, I pursued great opportunities and I made great money. I started several companies that were very successful. By age 23 I was well into the six figures in my income, and I made my first million dollars by age 27. While I am proud of that, my ambition came from a place of insecurity which caused me to work long hours. Long hours negatively affected my faith, family, and fitness.

As I think back to my pursuit of success and prosperity, I have to acknowledge that in my earlier years, I was driven by a desire to prove myself. This stemmed from my modest upbringing and childhood challenges. I grew up in Southern California. A lot of people hear 'Southern California' and think about places like Costa Mesa and Anaheim. Those are wonderful communities, and there might have been times when I wished I had grown up there. But the place I came from was very different from the seemingly carefree opulence of Orange County.

My hometown is Hemet, California. It's a city where many of the blue collar workers who built Southern California come from. It's a place where tradesmen and gangsters and immigrant communities live — mostly in single-story 1,500 square foot houses, or in mobile homes. I honor the hard working people of my hometown, but it was a place I couldn't wait to leave. I wanted to be somewhere else — somewhere that had more people, more money, and abundant opportunity. When I really think about it, my experience in Hemet put a spirit of scarcity in me. I was surrounded by people who were working hard but struggling to make ends meet. The general sense of lack was pervasive; it was like a disease and I caught it.

One man in the scriptures who started at the bottom and became a great 'man of means" and financial integrity is Joseph.

GOD'S MAN: JOSEPH

Joseph's story is one of perseverance, faith, poverty, abundance and humility. He was born in the ancient land of Canaan, and was the favorite son of his father, Jacob. However, his brothers became jealous of him and sold him into slavery in Egypt. Despite his difficult circumstances, Joseph remained faithful to God and used his gifts of dream interpretation and leadership to serve his master and rise to a position of great power in the Egyptian empire. You can read Joseph's story in Genesis chapters 37–50. Joseph was known for his wisdom, his honesty, and his unwavering trust in God, even in the face of great adversity. Joseph's wealth and position of influence allowed him to provide for his family — and a nation — during a time of famine. Ultimately, he preserved the line of Abraham and ensured that God's promise of a great nation would continue to be fulfilled. Joseph's story is a powerful reminder that even in the darkest of circumstances, God is always at work, and His plans and purposes will be accomplished. Through Joseph's financial integrity, wisdom, and obedience, God was able to bring about great good, and Joseph's life serves as a shining example of what it means to be a godly man of means who lives with financial integrity.

DIGGING DEEPER: JOSEPH

1   **Read Genesis 39:1–10.** What are some examples of how Joseph demonstrated integrity and hard work? How did Joseph's integrity seem to connect with his wisdom about money in his life? How did this benefit him and those around him?

2   **Read Genesis 39:11–23.** In what ways did Joseph's time in prison prepare him for his eventual rise to power in Egypt? How did his experience in prison shape his character and faith?

3   **Read Genesis 41:15–46.** What role did Joseph's ability to interpret dreams play in his life, and what does this tell us about the importance of relying on God's guidance and wisdom in our own lives? Summarize Joseph's financial wisdom from this passage of scripture — and what it led to.

4   **Read Genesis 41:47–57.** How did Joseph's approach to saving and investing during times of abundance reflect his understanding of God's sovereignty and provision? What can we learn from his example in our own financial management?

5   **Read Genesis 47:13–26.** How did Joseph's wealth and position of influence in Egypt allow him to fulfill God's purposes and provide for His people during a time of famine? What can we learn from Joseph's example of stewardship and generosity?

YOUR KINGDOM ASSIGNMENT: BECOME WEALTHY

John Wesley was a radical Christian revivalist in the 1700's. He reached a point where his personal income (mostly from book royalties) was 25 times that of an average workman — and he donated 90% of it to ministries. John's views on money and work were profound, summarized in this quote: "Earn all you can, save all you can, give all you can." This saying emphasizes the importance of earning money through hard work, being frugal and saving as much as possible, and then giving generously to others and to God's purposes. Wesley believed that financial stewardship was an essential aspect of Christian discipleship, and that by using our resources wisely and generously, we can be a blessing to others and help to advance God's kingdom on earth. While so much more can and should be said about the pursuit of financial integrity, I want to let those three elements serve as touchstones for your kingdom assignment with regard to financial integrity.

1. EARN ALL YOU CAN

"Lazy hands make for poverty, but diligent hands bring wealth"
Proverbs 10:4 NIV

As a Christian, you are called to work diligently and with integrity, using your God-given abilities to provide for yourself and your family, and to bless others through your work. By embracing the value of hard work and diligence, you can glorify God and make a positive impact in the world. Your industriousness, ambition, and drive can actually be used by God to create opportunity for economic advancement and abundance for all those you employ. This can and should also lead to prosperity for you as well. So go for it — and grind! But don't 'earn all you can' because you're concerned there won't be enough. Earn all you can because you know that with God, there will be more than enough! Earn your money ethically and legally and in a responsible way — but earn all you can!

2. SAVE ALL YOU CAN

"The wise store up choice food and olive oil, but fools gulp theirs down"
Proverbs 21:20 NIV

If you recall, part of the wisdom of Joseph was seen in the decision to store up 20% of the harvest, year after year. This allowed him to be in a position of wealth and strength when a cyclical financial downturn came along. God's Word teaches us the importance of being good stewards of our resources and using them wisely. By being frugal and wise in your financial management, you can be better prepared for times of need and better positioned to bless others through your generosity. You must avoid all high-rate consumer debt as well; pay off your credit card debt, and don't carry a balance on any card! Your savings and investments plan cannot be an afterthought. It must be part of your strategy for enjoying the resources God entrusts to you!

3. GIVE ALL YOU CAN

"Give, and it will be given to you. A good measure, pressed down, shaken together and running over, will be poured into your lap. For with the measure you use, it will be measured to you" Luke 6:38 NIV

Brother, you are called to be generous and compassionate, reflecting God's love and grace to others through your actions. By giving generously to others, you not only bless those in need but also experience the joy and abundance that comes from trusting in God's provision and grace. One of the wisest investments you can make is the investment of your tithe into your local church. To tithe means to take 10% of your income — every week or every month — and give it to your church. This is a principle and a practice the scriptures teach in Malachi 3:6–12. Don't mess with this! God's plan for blessing your finances starts with you faithfully bringing the first 10% of your income to His church so His church's mission can thrive. Give your gifts to missionaries and support for the poor above and beyond that tithe. Give to help people in need above and beyond that tithe. Watch for how the Lord is faithful to bless you as you obey this Kingdom principle!

MAN ARISE AS A MAN OF MEANS

I want you to become a Man of Means who creates value and earns money ethically, diligently, and abundantly. Become a saver, using prudence to be prepare for unforeseen headwinds. Once you earn all you can and save all you can, you will reach the most important step and you can give money away generously and abundantly to the Kingdom of God and those in need. As a Christian man, it is up to you to master money and not let it master you. By becoming a man of means, you will reflect the abundance and generosity of the God who has given you everything. You will leave in the peace of knowing provision comes from God and the joy of sharing it freely for God's purposes.

THE REST OF THE SKYLAR'S STORY

That sense of scarcity I developed in Hemet did serve me; it created a sense of drive and hunger in me that fueled my ambition as I launched company after company. On one hand, I'm grateful for the reality of growing up in a harder place, in a harder time, because it kept me from becoming soft. It lit a fire inside of me for pursuing better, pursuing more, for working hard to attain a better life. And I did attain a better life.

Nevertheless, as I have grown in my faith, I have come to understand that an abundance mindset is more helpful and empowering than a scarcity mindset. My understanding of the scripture is that God is generous, and that He is generous because He is the source of everything. He owns "the cattle on a thousand hills." In His generosity, God is willing to bless His children as we trust in Him — and He is willing to provide for us abundantly.

While I don't believe in a 'prosperity gospel', I do believe that scripture shows that generally, God leans towards empowering His children to experience prosperity as they fear Him and trust in Him. This is separate from "The Gospel." It is a principle that can be seen from the Old Testament to the New. From Abraham who had thousands of herds of animals — which was great wealth — to David and Solomon, to New Testament people such as Lydia in Philippi (Acts 16:13–15) and brother Barnabas (Acts 4:36–37), the scriptures show us one example after another of God giving an abundance to His sons and daughters as they work and trust Him. I also note that in most of these cases, the abundance God provides is used to establish God's Kingdom.

As I matured and pursued my goals, I had to grow in my thinking. I needed to shed the scarcity mentality that came from growing up in Hemet. I have retained the 'grit and grind it' gear that my place of upbringing gave me and I thank God for it. But I have embraced an abundance mentality based on a deep trust in the character of God, and based on an understanding of His desire for His people to build and establish great things for God's Kingdom and God's people. For any of us to do that, we must become a 'man of means' — and a man of financial integrity.

 KINGS DISCUSSION QUESTIONS

1   What is the general state of your financial affairs? Give yourself a letter grade for each of the three categories.

   Use one or two words to give the reason for why your 'grade' regarding finances is low — or high.

2   **Read Proverbs 22:29.** Are you using the skills and abilities God has given you to the best of your ability in your work? How can you better honor God in your job?

   Are you giving your work your all? Or are you 'mailing it in' in any way?

3   **Read Colossians 3:23–24.** What is your attitude toward work? Do you work as if you are serving the Lord, or are you more focused on earning money for your own purposes? Are you using the skills and abilities God has given you for building His Kingdom?

Share about a way you are taking your earning capacity — your work — for granted. Repent.

4   **Read Proverbs 21:20.** Do you see saving money as a way to be a good steward of the resources God has given you, or as a way to accumulate wealth for yourself? How can you balance saving for the future with being generous in the present?

Share about your actual money saving plan and strategy and actions and results — or failures.

5   **Read Proverbs 6:6–8.** In what areas of your life are you tempted to be wasteful or indulgent with your finances? How can you be more disciplined in your spending and saving habits?

Share the most recent wasteful purchase you made and why it was a fail.

6   **Read Luke 6:38.** How has your generosity reflected God's love and grace to others? In what ways can you use your resources to bless those in need and further God's kingdom?

Share about the most recent time you blessed or helped someone financially — directly. If you haven't, repent.

7   **Read Malachi 3:7–10 and 2 Corinthians 9:6–8.** What fears or doubts do you have about giving sacrificially to further God's Kingdom? How can you trust in God's provision and grace to overcome those fears and give generously?

Are you actually tithing? Yes or no? Not 'giving' but TITHING as defined above. Share why you want to disobey God with regards to this, and why your kingdom matters more than his. Yeah, that question stings, huh?

ARISE AND ACCEPT THE CHALLENGE

1   Put an extra $100 bill in your car and also in your wallet — specifically to give to someone in need like a great King would do. Find someone to give it to while out and about — NOT to someone who works for you.

2   Open up a new savings account — and set up an automatic transfer of a specific dollar amount every month. Determine that this savings account is for 'extra generosity beyond the tithe'.

3   Create a strategy for one more stream of income that you will work on establishing over the next six months.

4   Start tithing to your church — really tithing. See what God does, and report back.

A MAN
OF GOD

"God made him who had no sin to be sin for us,
so that in him we might become the righteousness of God."

2 Corinthians 5:21 NIV

JOHN'S STORY: LEARNING TO LIVE IN GODLINESS

When I was a middle school student, I did not know the Lord. My idea of a good time was going down to the beach with a friend, and competing to see how many girls we could hook up with in one night. On other occasions, the plan would be to do some drinking or do some drugs in as many interesting places as we could find. Sometimes we would have a competition of how many things we could steal from different stores in one night. After one weekend of extreme debauchery like this, I came home and could not fall asleep because my heart was racked with guilt. We had taken advantage of girls with these random hookups, and we had stolen so many things, and gotten ourselves as drunk as can be. It all finally hit me, and I felt gross and dirty. I remember lying on my bed with tears running down my cheeks. I couldn't shake the guilty feeling, and there was a dark, heavy cloud of shame hanging over my head.

That week, a guy from school named Mark invited me to his youth group. Of course I resisted, because I wasn't into that kind of thing. After several invitations, I caved in and I went to the youth group. At the end of the message, the youth pastor shared the simple gospel. He said, "If you want to receive the forgiveness of your sins, and the gift of salvation through Jesus Christ, you need to repent, and ask Jesus to forgive you, and surrender your life to Him. If you want to do that, would you raise your hand?" Almost involuntarily, my hand shot up. The next thing I knew, I was praying out loud asking Jesus to forgive my sins! I felt so much relief in that moment as God's goodness came into my heart. I was washed clean; I was set free from the guilt and shame of my sins! I received the gift of salvation; I was truly saved.

For a couple of months, I continued to go to that youth group. I learned more about Jesus and I experienced the goodness of connecting with other believers for worship. However, after a couple months, I drifted away. I started working at a part-time job and I was no longer able to go to the youth group meetings. I started hanging out with people from the job, and they took me backwards. I hadn't really gotten very closely connected with the believers in that youth group. This left me vulnerable and I backslid into sin, little by little. What I needed was to engage in real discipleship that would help me experience more of the sanctification that was deeply needed in my life. It is such a gift to be saved, but God's plan is always for people who are saved by Jesus to also be sanctified by Jesus. I needed to discover what it meant to not just be 'saved', but to truly become a man of God.

After we are saved and the burden of the penalty of sin is removed from our spirit, the Holy Spirit begins to dismantle the power of sin in our lives. We participate in this process of sanctification through the choice we make to move in the direction of righteousness and holiness. We fuel this process of sanctification through our engagement in spiritual disciplines-prayer, Bible reading, fasting, worship, fellowship with accountability, and others. These kinds of spiritual disciplines help us to change the way we think; they renew our minds. In turn, God does deep transformative work in our lives, changing us from the inside out. This is what Romans 12:2 indicates when it says, "Do not conform to the pattern of this world, but be transformed by the renewing of your mind."

GOD'S MAN: DAVID

King David is one of the most prominent figures in the Old Testament and a central character in the history of Israel. He was the youngest son of Jesse and was anointed by the prophet Samuel to be the next king of Israel, even as he was still a young shepherd boy. David rose to prominence as a warrior and military leader, defeating the giant Goliath with a sling and a stone, and later leading successful military campaigns against the enemies of Israel. He also became a skilled musician and songwriter, and is credited with composing many of the Psalms in the Bible. David is famous for his reign as king of Israel, and his rule is often described as a golden age in the history of the nation. He is remembered for his great accomplishments, such as his successful military campaigns, unifying the North and the South — Israel and Judah — his establishment of Jerusalem as the capital of Israel, and his commissioning of the building of the Temple. David is featured prominently in the books of Samuel and Chronicles, where his life and legacy are recounted in great detail. In the Rise Up Kings movement, we highly regard the example of King David. Throughout his life, David demonstrated a deep and abiding faith in and love for God, even amidst great personal struggles and challenges. He is known for his passionate love for the Lord, his heartfelt worship, and his unwavering trust in God's promises. David's faith was so strong that he was described as a man after God's own heart — despite his failures — and this is what you are meant to strive for as well.

DIGGING DEEPER: DAVID

1 **Read 1 Samuel 17:12–54.** In what ways did David's life reflect his faith and trust in God? What did his bold courage do for God's people? How did that set him up well for his future as King?

2 **Read 1 Samuel 18:1–4 and 1 Samuel 20:12–17.** How did David's relationship with Jonathan reflect his faith and commitment to God — and what value did that friendship give both men? What can you learn from David and Jonathan's example of godly friendship and loyalty, and how can you apply this to your relationships with other brothers?

3 **Read 2 Samuel 11:1–15 and Psalm 51.** How did David's sin with Bathsheba and subsequent repentance impact his relationship with God? What can you learn from David's example of humility and repentance in response to sin, and how can you apply this to your own life?

4 **Read 2 Samuel 5:10 and 2 Samuel 7:1–17.** What can you learn from David's example of unwavering trust in God's promises, even in the face of adversity? In what ways did David's leadership as king reflect his faith and obedience to God? What can you learn from David's example of humble leadership and obedience to God's will? How can you apply this to your own leadership roles?

YOUR KINGDOM ASSIGNMENT: BECOME GODLY!

I want to challenge you to embrace your identity as a man of God — and to make choices in keeping with what it means to be just that! Being a man of God is to embody the character of Christ in all aspects of life. Live a life led by the Holy Spirit and obedient to God's will. It means being transformed from the inside out, with a heart that beats for God's purposes and a mind that is set on things above. It means being a loving husband, a devoted father, a faithful friend, and a humble lover of God. It embraces the challenges and trials of life with faith, hope, and courage, knowing that God is with you every step of the way. As a man of God, you are called to lead by example, to inspire others to follow Christ, and to leave a legacy of faith that will last for generations. While I could go on to give further definition to what it means to be a man of God, I want to give you God's Word on the matter — and I'll let this one verse from 1 Timothy 6:11 serve as the underpinning for your Kingdom assignment: "But you, man of God, flee from all this, and pursue righteousness, godliness, faith, love, endurance, and gentleness." The pursuit of these six marks of a man of God is your Kingdom assignment!

1. RISE UP IN RIGHTEOUSNESS

"The integrity of the upright guides them, but the unfaithful are destroyed by their duplicity." Proverbs 11:3 NIV

As a Christian, you have positional righteousness through your faith in Jesus; you are in the position of righteousness before God because of the Cross of Christ. You have received God's gift of salvation. At the same time, you are a disciple of Jesus who is growing in a process called sanctification — and that means you are learning to choose practical righteousness through your actions. God responds to this obedience by giving you power by the Holy Spirit to resist sinful desires. He allows your redeemed spirit within you to give birth to good, noble desires and to have the will to act on them. As a man of God, you are called to live a life of integrity and uprightness. You must be honest in your dealings with others and seek to do what is right, even when it is difficult. Proverbs 21:3 says, "To do righteousness and justice is more acceptable to the Lord than sacrifice." This means that your actions matter to God, and He is pleased when you choose to do what is right, even if it is not the easy path.

2. GROW MORE IN GODLINESS

"Train yourself for godliness; for while bodily training is of some value, godliness is of value in every way, as it holds promise for the present life and also for the life to come." 1 Timothy 4:7b–8

Godliness is the manifestation of the Holy Spirit's work in a man's life, transforming him into the likeness of Christ. It is a real love for God, a deep and abiding reverence for His Word, and an unwavering devotion to His will. Godliness includes your decision to live by the spirit — and not by the flesh. So you must grow to recognize the difference between the two. Recognizing the difference between the desires or impulses of the flesh — and the desires of your new nature is vital for spiritual health. Your spiritual health is as important as your physical health, and you must make it a priority in your life. When you prioritize your relationship and times of encounter with God, you will become more like Him, and your spiritual vitality will sustain you and inspire others.

3. FIRE UP YOUR FAITH

"Now faith is confidence in what we hope for and assurance about what we do not see." Hebrews 11:1 NIV

Being a man of faith means living a life of purpose and commitment to God, knowing that every step you take is guided by His divine hand. As a man of faith, you trust in God's wisdom and sovereignty, knowing that He is always faithful to His promises and that His plans for you are good. You also understand that faith is not just a matter of belief but a matter of action, and that you are called to live out your faith in every area of your life, including your relationships, work, and community. As a man of faith, you are empowered by the Holy Spirit to live a life of courage, taking bold risks as you sense God leading you; a life of compassion, offering support and love to your family and those in need; and a life of hope, trusting in God's goodness, even when your circumstances may seem bleak.

4. LIVE OUT THE LOVE

"Dear friends, let us love one another, for love comes from God. Everyone who loves has been born of God and knows God."
1 John 4:7 NIV

A strong, godly man embraces love as one of his highest ideals. As a man of love, you are empowered by the Holy Spirit to love as Christ loves. You are called to love sacrificially, just as Christ laid down His life for us. You are called to love unconditionally, just as Christ loves us despite our flaws and imperfections. And you are called to love extravagantly, overflowing with the love of God that has been poured into your heart by the Holy Spirit. Choose to love God and others with all your heart, soul, mind, and strength. Allow the Holy Spirit to empower you to love sacrificially, unconditionally, and extravagantly. And know that as you love, you are fulfilling the greatest commandment and bringing glory to God's name.

5. ENGAGE WITH ENDURANCE

"God blesses those who patiently endure testing and temptation. Afterward they will receive the crown of life that God has promised to those who love him." James 1:12 NLT

Brother, you must persevere through difficult times, knowing that God is with you every step of the way. This is the essence of endurance. You must endure challenges and hardships, knowing that God is using them to shape you into the man He wants you to be. As a man of endurance, you understand that life is not always easy, and you will face obstacles, but you are empowered by the Holy Spirit to keep going, even when things get tough. To live a life of endurance, you must keep your focus on God and His promises. You must trust in His faithfulness and love, and believe that He will never leave you or forsake you. You must also seek His guidance and wisdom, knowing that He will direct your steps and guide you through any situation. You must not give up or lose heart, but continue to press on toward the goal that God has set before you. Look at the obstacles, and grit on with it! That's right — grit on with it!

As we say at Rise Up Kings, difficulty in life doesn't happen to us, it happens for us!

6. GENERATE REAL GENTLENESS

"Let your gentleness be evident to all. The Lord is near."
Philippians 4:5 NIV

Gentleness means showing kindness, humility, and grace in your interactions with others, even in challenging situations. As a man of God who pursues gentleness, you understand that your strength and power are to be used to serve and care for others, not to dominate or control. To live a life of gentleness, you must first understand that it is a fruit of the Holy Spirit. You must be filled with the Spirit and allow Him to transform you from the inside out. You must also be willing to submit to God's will and follow His example of gentleness the way you see it in Jesus. Gentleness does not mean weakness. It's actually the opposite of weakness. Gentleness, or meekness, is great power under great control. Imagine a bodybuilder tenderly holding a baby. That is you: powerful and gentle with those who are weaker than you.

MAN ARISE AS A MAN OF GOD

To be a man of God means that you are someone who is secure in God's love for you, and you are motivated by your love for God. As a man of God, you seek to align your thoughts, words, and actions with the character of Jesus Christ, and live your life in the power of the Holy Spirit. It means that you stand firm in your faith, no matter the circumstances or challenges that come your way. You are a man of God — you express and act on the spiritual authority and power that are available to you through the resurrection of Christ. You live and lead with integrity, compassion, strength, and humility. Your love for God is evident to others and is infused into everything you do.

You might be thinking to yourself, "But I'm not perfect. I'm flawed, I make mistakes." And that's okay. None of us are perfect. We all stumble and fall at times. But what sets a man of God apart is that he is willing to get back up and keep going. He doesn't give up when the going gets tough. He perseveres through challenges and learns from his mistakes.

So, what does a man of God do? He truly loves the Lord his God with all his heart; he loves his family, his friends, and his neighbors. He serves his community, seeking to make a positive impact in the lives of those around him. He leads with humility, seeking to understand the needs and perspectives of others. He takes responsibility for his actions, and he admits when he's wrong. He seeks wisdom from God and from those who have gone before him.

But let me be clear: being a man of God is not about being weak or passive. It's not about being a doormat or a pushover. No, a man of God is strong, courageous, and bold. He stands up for what he believes in, even when it's not popular or easy. He fights for justice and for the rights of the oppressed. He is a defender of truth and of the weak. So, brother, I want to encourage you to be a man of God. It's not an easy path, but it's a fulfilling one. It's a path that leads to joy, purpose, and meaning. It's a path that leaves a positive legacy for generations to come. It's the path that King David walked. Let's discover more together about the life of King David.

THE REST OF JOHN'S STORY

I wish I could tell you that after that sinful weekend at the beach and the moment in youth group where I got saved, I've only walked in holiness and godliness. That isn't the case. That moment of receiving the gift of salvation created the starting point of a real relationship with God. That day I was saved. But I am still being sanctified and that process will continue in me until I'm in heaven. That day I began a journey of a life with Jesus. I have needed to choose a life of godliness. I needed to learn what it means to be a man of God.

In my journey of growing as a godly man, I've had to learn how to give my affection to God, how to apply the scriptures in my day-to-day life, and how to advance my engagement with the spiritual disciplines that fuel my growth in godliness. I've had to come to Jesus again and again, not for salvation, but for new mercy in an area where it has become clear that I've fallen short of God's standard. For example, in one season, I was operating with so much selfishness in my marriage, and that sin was something God had to deal with me about. In another season, lust became more of a struggle than it had been before. God brought conviction and correction to me about that, and I had to choose to change my patterns to grow in godliness. In another moment of my life, unbridled anger was becoming a huge problem for me, and it was a sin in God's eyes. I had to work on it, through counseling, inner healing prayer, and accountability.

There have been — and continue to be aspects of my life that need adjustment so that I grow in being a man of God. In all these moments, I've found that if I will humble myself, repent, and apply myself to making a change, He empowers me by the Spirit to do it. The result is that for several decades now I've continued to take one step after another toward a more godly life. The brutal reality is that sometimes the journey is two steps forward, then one step back (or three?). But the direction and the trendline is toward an increase of godliness in my life, through the mercies of God that are new every morning (Lamentations 3:23). I am grateful for every moment I've confessed my sin, repented, taken communion with a contrite heart, and committed my steps again to the Way of Jesus. And I am grateful for the Cross because it stands for all eternity as a sentinel declaring that I am loved and forgiven! That truth gives me the power to keep going and to keep growing in godliness!

 KINGS DISCUSSION QUESTIONS

1   When it comes to being a man of God, how are things going for you, based on what you read in this chapter? Give yourself a letter grade (A+ to F-) and say why.

   What is the one thing keeping you from really being a man of God? Why do you feel you can't be or have failed at being a man of God?

2   **Read Proverbs 11:3 and Proverbs 11:5–6.** Describe how you have sought to live a life of righteousness marked by integrity and honesty, even when it may not be easy or convenient. Share about a time when you have been challenged to compromise your values, but chose to remain true to what you believe.

   In what way are you currently facing (or have recently faced) a temptation to throw away your practical righteousness? Name what it is, and the steps you are taking to flee from it.

3   **Read 1 Timothy 4:7–8 and Titus 2:11–13.** What have you learned about what godliness is, and what practices could help you grow in godliness?

🛡 *What kind of ungodliness have you demonstrated or lived out recently? You need to be honest about this — so that you can grow beyond it!*

4   **Read Galatians 2:20 and 2 Corinthians 5:7.** How has your faith in Jesus sustained you during challenging times? How can we cultivate a deeper faith that extends beyond just attending church or reading the Bible?

🛡 *What actions are you currently taking to deepen, strengthen and live out your Christian faith, and take your walk with Jesus to the next level? What areas of your life are you NOT including God in? Why?*

5   **Read 1 Corinthians 13:2–7.** In what ways do you show love to those around you, even to those who may not be easy to love? Read John 15:12–13. How can we practice sacrificial love as Christ did, and what does that look like in your daily life?

🛡 *Name three people who are relationally connected to you, and guess what score THEY would give you regarding how loving you are, on a scale of 1–10. What adjustments do you need to make to truly live out more love?*

6 **Read Hebrews 12:1–2 and James 1:12.** What are some ways that you have developed endurance in your faith? How can we encourage each other to persevere through difficult circumstances and not give up on our faith?

> Name some of the triggers that make you want to quit the good and noble things in your life.

7 **Read Philippians 4:5, Ephesians 4:2, and Galatians 5:22–23.** What are some practical ways that we can cultivate gentleness in our interactions with others? How do you balance gentleness with assertiveness when standing up for what you believe in? How can you speak what you believe with both conviction AND humility?

> Share about a time you've failed at living out gentleness recently and diagnose why that happened — and what you're going to do about it.

ARISE AND ACCEPT THE CHALLENGE

1 Immediately confess any known sin in your life to at least one Christian brother, and ask that brother if you could do this daily or weekly.

2 Go to your church service or find one to attend and, during worship, open your mouth and actually sing, even lift your hands in worship. Do something bold in worship like King David did in 2 Samuel 6:14!

3 Establish a big, audacious goal for your enterprise and take a first step toward it.

4 Create a 'quit-list.' Name the ungodly, foolish, time-wasting things you're going to quit! Write that list down in several places where you'll be reminded! When you feel like quitting, focus on THIS quit list!

A MAN OF PHYSICAL STRENGTH

"It is God who arms me with strength and keeps my way secure."

Psalm 18:32 NIV

JOHN'S STORY:
DISCOVERING THE IMPORTANCE OF MAXIMIZED PHYSICALITY

A few years ago, I was pastoring and walking through a tough season of life with a brother in our church. A recent affair had almost crashed and burned his marriage. Eric and I struck up a friendship through the process of him and his wife working through the aftermath of that affair. Eric is 6'4" and built like a Mr. Universe. He's the kind of guy that other men see and respect instantly, at least for the sheer impressiveness of his physical presence. Eric suggested that he and I meet at the gym and work out together. My first thought was 'heck no!'. Who was I to be working out with a guy like this? But I agreed, and we met at the gym.

Eric taught me proper exercise techniques and it was the first time in my life I'd learned anything about proper structure, correct form, and effective approach to muscle isolation. Even though it was four years ago, I can still hear him in my ear: "Structure, structure, John!" He had put his bear-paw-sized hands on my shoulders and repositioned my form to reflect the kind of healthy posture that a strong man should possess: chest out, shoulders back, legs squared up, neck elongated. I literally felt stronger just being nearby Eric — and my body was learning an appropriate kind of stature that would be healthy and safe for the muscle building that would follow.

Eric taught me the proper form for each exercise so I wouldn't damage my body. He helped me understand the value of sequence and which kinds of exercises paired well together. Each time we met at the gym, he came with a complete one-hour workout set written out and ready to go. All I had to do was go along for the ride. I was so excited about the results. When we started I was benching a measly 135 pounds. After a couple of months with Eric, I was benching 205 and I was enjoying similar gains on all the other muscle groups. My back muscles were stronger than they'd ever been in my life; I had even achieved the elusive 'V' from the lats down to the waist.

In the scriptures, the images of God's people Israel going to war always captivates me. You read about tens of thousands of people — men of God — marching against another army. There are no drones, no tanks. It's just bodies, shields, swords, and human strength. Sheer human strength. Think about the size of the temple in Jerusalem and how it was made; the stones were set in place by the sheer strength of human beings whose bodies were agile and healthy! One of the people in the Bible who is known for his admirable strength is Samson. Let's discover more together about the life of Samson.

GOD'S MAN: SAMSON

The record of Samson is found in the book of Judges, specifically in chapters 13–16. His story is set during a time in Israel's history known as the period of the judges, which is estimated to be between 1200 and 1000 BC. During this time, the Israelites were in a cycle of sin, oppression, repentance, and deliverance; they would turn away from God, be oppressed by their enemies, cry out to God for help, and then be delivered by a judge whom God raised up.

Samson was one of these judges, chosen by God from birth to be a deliverer of Israel. He was a Nazirite, meaning he was consecrated to God from birth and had to follow certain rules, including not cutting his hair, not drinking alcohol, and not touching anything unclean. Samson was known for his incredible strength, which he used to defeat Israel's enemies, the Philistines. He was given the title of "judge" because he acted as a leader and protector of the Israelites. But Samson was not without his flaws. He was often tempted by women and had a weakness for them. Samson had made Nazirite vows to avoid such things as touching dead bodies. While technically he took honey from a lion's carcass, he brought himself extremely close to the edge. Samson's story serves as a reminder of the consequences of sin and disobedience to God, as well as the power of redemption and repentance. It also highlights the importance of staying true to one's vows and the dangers of giving in to temptation. As Christian men, we can learn from Samson's strengths and weaknesses, and strive to live a life that is pleasing to God, even in the face of temptation. Read all of Judges 13–17 if you can, and reference the passages below as you dig deeper.

DIGGING DEEPER: SAMSON

1   **Read Judges 14:5–9.** How did Samson's reaction to the lion reflect his faith and relationship with God? What can we learn from his response to the situation? Did Samson stay true to his commitment to never touch anything unclean (like an animal carcass)?

2   **Read Judges 14:1–4, 10–20.** How did Samson's disobedience to his parents and disregard for God's commands lead to negative consequences in his life? What can we learn from this story about the importance of honoring those whom God has placed over us and following God's will?

3   **Read Judges 15:14–17.** Samson used the jawbone of a donkey to defeat 1,000 Philistines. What can we learn from this story about the power of God and the importance of having and using our strength to serve Him?

4   **Read Judges 16:15–17.** How did Samson's actions reflect a lack of trust in God, and how did they lead to his downfall? What can we learn from his mistakes, and how can we apply these lessons in our own lives?

5   **Read Judges 16:21–30.** How did Samson's sacrifice reflect his commitment to God and his willingness to do whatever it takes to serve Him? What can we learn from his ultimate act of faith and obedience to God?

YOUR KINGDOM ASSIGNMENT: BECOME A MAN OF PHYSICAL STRENGTH

Brother, as you seek to live a life of purpose and fulfillment for the glory of God, don't neglect the importance of your physical health. Your earthly purpose will be accomplished through the one and only earthly vessel you've got: your body. Even if your primary work and contribution is mental, your mental state and capacity will either be complemented and supported — or diminished — by your physical state. God has entrusted you with your body, and it is your responsibility to take care of it. There are three crucial dynamics of physical health that you must prioritize in your daily life: diet and nutrition, physical exercise, and stretching.

1. GIVE YOUR BODY GOOD NUTRITION!

"Don't you realize that your body is the temple of the Holy Spirit, who lives in you and was given to you by God? You do not belong to yourself, for God bought you with a high price. So you must honor God with your body." 1 Corinthians 6:19–20 NLT

Your diet and nutrition play a critical role in your physical health. Your body needs a balanced and varied diet to function at its best. Eat a diet full of fruits, vegetables, whole grains, lean proteins, and healthy fats, while limiting processed and sugary foods. You should understand that in Bible times, there wasn't even such a thing as processed sugar — just honey; and even that was recommended to be eaten with limitations. Our bodies just weren't designed to process the amount of sugar and processed carbohydrates our modern American diet typically provides. It's time to make some changes! Evaluate your caloric intake, and generally avoid consuming more calories than you need based on your body size. Consider engaging in intermittent fasting in order to provide your body a chance to cleanse itself. Back off on the alcohol consumption and eliminate the use of non-prescription drugs from your body!

2. DO A DAILY WORKOUT AS A DIVINE DISCIPLINE!

"Physical training is good, but training for godliness is much better, promising benefits in this life and in the life to come." 1 Timothy 4:8 NIV

Regular physical exercise is essential for good health — but brother, I know you know this! Regular exercise not only benefits your physical health, but it can also improve your mental health and reduce stress. Make it a priority to get at least 30 minutes of moderate exercise each day. This could include walking, running, cycling, weightlifting, or any other activity that gets your heart rate up. You should continue to build those muscles. Don't you want to be the guy who can lift someone's heavy suitcase for them without worrying about your back? Don't you want to be that man who can carry that heavy piece of furniture to help your neighbor? Of course you do! So keep putting a priority on your physical exercise! Let your physical workout be as much a priority to you as your spiritual devotional life. You're not working out for vanity's sake; you're working out to serve the Lord as well as you can for as long as you can!

3. DON'T SKIP THE STRETCHING!

"I discipline my body like an athlete, training it to do what it should." 1 Corinthians 9:27

Don't overlook the importance of stretching. Stretching can help prevent injuries, reduce muscle soreness, and improve your flexibility. Stretching is a form of discipline that helps you care for your body and improve your physical performance. Make sure to incorporate stretching into your daily routine, either before or after exercise, or even as a separate activity on its own. Our lifespans are longer than they were in the times of King David and Jesus. That means we need to give extra attention to the issue of our elasticity. As our bodies get older, they can tend to become a bit more brittle. But 'motion is lotion' for the inner workings of the body. Keep yours going for God's glory for as long as you can, brother!

MAN ARISE AS A MAN OF PHYSICAL STRENGTH

Brother, I want to challenge you to see your body as a gift from God and to determine that you WILL tend well to it. I want you to catch a vision for having the capacity to run around with your grandkids one day — full of strength and vitality, not worn out and out of shape. It can happen! But you've got to decide to MAKE it happen! Your physical body is the carriage through which you will experience your existence. Your physiological condition will, in many ways, determine — or at least strongly affect — your quality of life. You also may come up against physical problems you didn't ask for and can't take away. So to whatever degree you can take care of your body, you must!

When you consider the people in the Bible, you have to understand that most of them spent the majority of life engaged in physical exercise. They were walking everywhere they went, and they were farming, hunting, building, and warring... so the scriptures written in their time would largely assume a healthy physicality. But our modern way of life has us on our rear a majority of the time, tempted to slurp down sugar water and pound carbs all day long while we're at it. This is NOT God's plan or design for our bodies, and we need to make some adjustments to how we live so that our physicality matches our spirituality (assuming our spiritual life is in tune)!

THE REST OF JOHN'S STORY

Around the same time as I was working out with Eric, I had a series of medical appointments that revealed troubling issues. To make a long story short, I had a tumor the size of an olive growing inside my spinal cord — and it had to be removed. The surgery would entail a double laminectomy and surgery through the dura of the spinal cord into the very fibers of the nerve bundle. The surgeon who evaluated me was optimistic. He said, "This is going to be a very critical surgery, and the recovery is going to be brutal. But, because of your physical strength, I think you are going to do just fine." He explained that because I had strong muscle tone and excellent health otherwise, the prognosis for recovery was much greater than it would otherwise have been.

I did go through with the surgery — and the recovery truly was brutal. The dura of the spinal cord is not meant to be opened, and strange things happen when it is. After the surgery, I lost my mobility for at least four weeks — and I couldn't walk, I couldn't pee, and for the first seven days, I couldn't defecate (I was trying to keep it clean — but what I mean is,

I couldn't even take a crap!). All I could think was, how bad would this have been if I hadn't been taking care of my body through good diet and exercise before this? I did eventually recover and that's a miraculous story in and of itself.

Because I deal with a physical condition that leaves me susceptible to the growth of Schwannoma tumors in my central and peripheral nervous system, I do NOT take physical health for granted. I have major health problems that I cannot do much about, and that motivates me to do all I can about those things I CAN do something about. I believe that our Heavenly Father gave us all things. Romans 11:36 (NLT) literally says as much and more: "For everything comes from him and exists by his power and is intended for his glory. All glory to him forever! Amen." This includes your physical body! And because your physical body is intended for His glory, you have a responsibility to figure out how to treat it well! This includes your diet, your posture, your physical exercise, and more.

 KINGS DISCUSSION QUESTIONS

1   How's your physical health these days — generally speaking? Are you taking good care of your body?

> *Talk about a time in your life when your body was at its best and why that was the case; discuss a step you could take to move towards that kind of health again.*

2   **Read 1 Corinthians 3:16–17 and 2 Corinthians 7:1.** Think about what you are putting into your body in light of these verses. Is what you consume destroying and damaging your body? What kinds of things do you need to stop ingesting because they are damaging or contaminating your body?

> *Name the most recent terrible 'food' you put into your body and how much of it you consumed. Describe your understanding of what it does to you to put that kind of thing into your body.*

3   **Read Romans 12:1 and 1 Timothy 4:8.** What are you doing to prepare your body to present it to God? What are your current patterns of physical exercise?

> *Share any sense of conviction you are currently experiencing about a change that needs to be made in your physical exercise.*

4   **Read Ecclesiastes 3:1.** I know it's a stretch (haha) but consider why stretching (even though the word isn't in the Bible) could be a vital daily discipline — and why it might matter to God.

> *Talk about a body concern or potential problem with your physical body that you are troubled by or afraid of.*

ARISE AND ACCEPT THE CHALLENGE

1   Go home and remove all junk food from your cabinets. Throw it in the trash, take a picture of it, and share it with some other kings.

2   Register for a gym membership and text a buddy to make a plan to work out together.

3   Find three different stretching guides on YouTube and create a stretching routine.

A MAN WHO
STANDS TALL

Do you see a man who excels in his work?

He will stand before kings; He will not stand before unknown men.

Proverbs 22:29 NKJV

JOHN'S STORY:
SEEING STATURE IN MEN WHO HAVE GONE BEFORE ME

I (John) have a personal legacy of men in my family who have done great things and stood tall in their communities. My great (to the 5th) grandfather on my mother's side was Hannibal Hamlin, Vice President to Abraham Lincoln. My grandfather on my mom's side was a soldier in WW2, and told stories about being in the trenches in North Africa, fighting for our freedom. He didn't even meet his daughter (my mother) until she was two years old because he was in the war. My grandfather on my dad's side was a United States congressman from Iowa. My uncle on my dad's side flew jets off of aircraft carriers in the Navy, and now owns and runs a large sales company that employs 150 people. My own father served on the church Board and city committees, while also running businesses and working as a lawyer. I am so blessed to be surrounded by the legacies of men of stature and good standing on both sides of my family tree.

There are few things more important than living a life that honors God and serves others. One way to do this is through public service, such as serving on boards, committees, coaching, or leading a business. Not only does this type of service help to demonstrate your Christian faith, but it can also be a powerful way to build a good reputation and standing in the community. Sometimes you forge the path into the opportunities to be a man of standing. Sometimes those opportunities just find you. That was the case for God's man, Daniel, in the Bible. Let's discover more about him!

GOD'S MAN: DANIEL

Daniel was a prominent figure in the Bible and a man of great faith. He was a Jew who was taken captive by the Babylonians during their conquest of Jerusalem in 597 BC. Despite being a captive, he rose to great prominence in the Babylonian court due to his wisdom, integrity, and devotion to God. Daniel interpreted dreams for the king and was also able to explain mysterious writing on a wall. He was known for his ability to interpret visions and prophecies, many of which related to the future of Israel and the coming of the Messiah. Throughout his life, Daniel remained committed to his faith, even when faced with persecution and threats to his life. He refused to compromise his beliefs and continued to pray to God even when it was forbidden. His faith and unwavering devotion to God set an example for others to follow. Daniel's life demonstrated that it is possible to remain true to one's beliefs even in the face of adversity, and that God will reward those who remain faithful to Him. His story continues to inspire believers today, reminding us of the power of faith in God and the importance of standing firm in the face of opposition.

DIGGING DEEPER: DANIEL

1   **Read Daniel 1:1–21.** What stands out to you about Daniel from this passage? What is your reaction to Daniel's decision to refuse the king's food and wine? What does this passage reveal about God's faithfulness to those who remain committed to Him?

2   **Read Daniel 2:46–48 and discuss.** What is the relationship between Daniel's work and the results? How does what happened for Daniel inspire you regarding your own future steps?

3   **Read Daniel 6:1–3.** What were the elements of Daniel's life that set him apart? What did Daniel's unselfishness and diligence lead to? What does a man need to do to be like Daniel in this regard?

4 **Read Daniel 6:4–28.** What can a man expect to experience if he moves into being a man of standing in the community? How are you motivated by Daniel's commitment to prayer, even when it was forbidden? How did God show his faithfulness to Daniel, and what was Daniel's part in that?

YOUR KINGDOM ASSIGNMENT: BECOME RESPECTED

As a Christian man, becoming a man of good standing in the community is not just a concept, but a way of being. It's about embodying the values and character traits that are essential to making a positive impact on those around you. By living an industrious life and being committed to community engagement, service, and leadership, you can become a role model and an influencer in your community. This doesn't mean you have to be perfect or have all the answers, but it does require a commitment to growth and a willingness to take initiative in your own enterprises, your community, and your church. By seeking out opportunities to serve, listening to the needs of those around you, and investing in the lives of others, you can build a reputation as a man of high standing in your community. This kind of living can have a powerful impact, not just on the people around you, but on future generations as well. So strive to be a man of high standing in all that you do, not for your own glory, but to honor God and make a positive impact on the world.

1. BE INDUSTRIOUS

"You have given him dominion over the works of your hands; you have put all things under his feet, all sheep and oxen, and also the beasts of the field, the birds of the heavens, and the fish of the sea, whatever passes along the paths of the seas." Psalm 8:6–8 NIV

You must choose to be industrious with your endeavors and strive to create value for the world. God has called us to be stewards of His creation, using our talents and resources to make the world a better place. By working hard and creating value, we can contribute to society, help those in need, and make a positive impact on the world. Furthermore, being industrious and creating value is a way of honoring God and fulfilling His purpose for our lives. When we use our abilities to make a difference, we demonstrate the love of Christ and share the Good News with those around us. So, whether it's in your business, your career, your hobbies, or your relationships, strive to be industrious and use your gifts. Remember, the work you do matters, and by creating value, you can leave a lasting legacy and honor God in all that you do.

2. BE A SERVANT IN THE COMMUNITY

"For even the Son of Man came not to be served but to serve others and to give his life as a ransom for many." Matthew 20:28 NLT

God intends for you to be a servant in your community, always seeking opportunities to volunteer and help those in need. Whether it's serving the poor, helping faithfully on a team in your church, or lending a hand in a community service project, your willingness to serve reflects the heart of Jesus Christ. In a world that often values power and success, choosing to be a servant may not always be easy, but it is a powerful way to demonstrate the love of Christ and make a positive impact in your community. Look for opportunities to volunteer! Join someone's initiative to make the city a better place. Place special emphasis on volunteering in your church. Join a team at church that builds up the church because we need our churches to be healthy and strong! Join an outreach experience with your church when there are opportunities to improve the community. That allows the church to add value to the community as it should. Be a part of that!

3. BE A LEADER IN YOUR COMMUNITY

"Seek the peace and prosperity of the city to which I have carried you into exile. Pray to the Lord for it, because if it prospers, you too will prosper." Jeremiah 29:7 NIV

You have a unique opportunity to be a positive force for change in your community by being a leader who guides and directs others toward the common good. Your local city, your county, your state, and even your country are always in need of those who would step forward with the capacity to lead. Brother, you should consider doing just that. Leadership is not about seeking power or control, but about using your gifts and abilities to serve others and make a difference in their lives, to affect positive, godly outcomes for the community. Seek opportunities to serve on committees and boards where you can use your skills and experiences to influence policies and decisions that will benefit the community and guide it toward godliness. Strong leadership is also essential for the health and strength of the church, where you can use your talents to inspire and guide others to follow Christ. There are teams and boards in your church that need you to make yourself available and committed to lead!

"For even the Son of Man came not to be served but to serve, and to give his life as a ransom for many." Mark 10:45 NLT

MAN ARISE AS A MAN OF RESPECT

Brother, you have everything it takes to be a man of stature. God has empowered you to rule and reign in the spheres of influence He has given you! A godly man of stature uses his influence to bless the lives of those around him. He uses his voice, his means, his influence to make every institution more effective: his church, his government, his children's schools. God did not put you in your position to shrink back from the important responsibility of using your stature for the good of others and the glory of God!

THE REST OF JOHN'S STORY

The rich family history I shared earlier has created in me an innate passion to be such a man myself. No one had to tell me I should; it's the product of growing up in an environment where that was the norm. In each of those men's lives, there is a personal history of hustle and grind that got them to their goals. NONE of them were handed their standing on a silver platter. They had to work for it, to fight for it, to choose for it. In my gut, I know that every single day I must do that as well. The goal is to live as a man who stands tall in the community, to be a man of stature.

Being a Christian man who has a good reputation, good stature, and good standing in the community is not an easy task. It requires intentionality, purposeful living, and a steadfast commitment to living out the values that define a Christian man. But with integrity, humility, courage, compassion, and faithfulness, it is possible to be a man of great character and influence, one who makes a positive difference in the lives of others and the world around you.

KINGS DISCUSSION QUESTIONS

1   Assess yourself in each of the three categories below on a scale of 1–10.
    How are you doing at being industrious?
    How are you doing being a servant in your community?
    How are you doing being a leader in the community?

Where did you rate the lowest, why, and what is your plan to improve on this?

2   **Read Colossians 3:23–24 and Psalm 8:6–8.** In what ways have you added value to the world through your work or other contributions? Share about a specific example where you have used your skills and resources to make a positive impact on others.

What has it cost you to be as industrious as you have been? Do you have any regrets about that?

3   **Read Galatians 5:13 and Matthew 20:28.** Describe how you have
    served others in your community and in your church. How can you
    give sacrificially of your time, talents, or resources to help someone in
    need, build up the community, or volunteer in a committed way?

    🛡 *If you haven't done anything like this in a while, why not?*
       Describe the kind of man you will be and be known as if you do
       not prioritize serving in the community.

4   **Read Philippians 2:3–4 and Galatians 2:20.** How have you sought to
    cultivate a heart of humility and service towards others, following the
    example of Christ? Share about a time when you have put others'
    needs before your own, or have chosen to serve in a way that was
    behind the scenes or unrecognized.

    🛡 *How do your ego and insecurities get in the way of you being a*
       servant? If so, what's the solution?

5   **Read 1 Timothy 3:1–7 and Matthew 5:16.** How have you demonstrated
    initiative in providing leadership in your city or church? Share about
    a specific instance where you have taken action to guide or influence
    others towards a positive outcome.

Describe the future of your city, county, or state if no men of God step up to serve in a public capacity. What is keeping you from stepping up to serve in a more official way?

6 **Read Romans 13:1.** What are some unique challenges that could come with serving in public office? How can we navigate them with integrity and grace?

7 **Read Micah 6:8.** How can we be effective leaders in our communities, even if we never hold public office?

ARISE AND ACCEPT THE CHALLENGE

1   Reach out to a pastor or leader in your church and ask to begin serving on a team in your church.

2   Sign up for the next city outreach, city clean-up day, or short-term mission trip that your church is doing.

3   Contact your local city government to discover how a citizen can join a commission or board and express interest. Ask to serve in that capacity.

4   Meet with a city council member, county leader, state legislator, etc., and ask them about ways to get involved in civic life.

A MAN FREE
FROM PORNOGRAPHY

*"I made a covenant with my eyes not to look lustfully
at a young woman."*

Job 31:1 NIV

JOHN'S STORY: INNOCENCE LOST

I was ten years old when I (John) moved to Princeton Junction, New Jersey. I was excited to explore the neighborhood. I had made friends with Justin, a kid who lived part-time with his mom just a couple blocks away. On a Saturday morning, I rode my bike over to Justin's house and he wasn't home. But the neighbor had done some serious 'spring cleaning' and there was a huge pile of trash by the curb — but some of it looked interesting. There was a TV, a chair, a desk, and some boxes of magazines. I had to investigate these treasures!

In the 80's, magazines were a big deal, so I started rifling through the box. Within seconds, I found there was a stack of Hustler, Penthouse, and Playboy magazines. I had never seen anything like this before and my eyes were glued to every single image I was seeing. The images totally captivated me and I wanted to see more. I grabbed a stack of them and shoved them into my backpack before Justin's mom came around the corner in her Ford Escort. Justin jumped out and I got him to come check out the treasures in the trash pile. When his mom went into the house, I said, "Dude, you have to check these out!" and I showed him the magazines. We looked at them a bit, wide-eyed and jaws dropped. We were ten years old and the last time either of us had seen anything like this was when we were breastfeeding as babies. He took a stack too and snuck them into his house.

I rode home later that day and stowed my special magazines under my mattress and in my closet. Over the next few days, after bedtime, I would get out from under the covers, turn on a flashlight, and turn to page after page of illicit imagery. There were elegant poses highlighting beauty and feminine form. There were seductive compositions in which her naked body and the look on her face seemed to say "You know you want me!" The sultry positions of self-pleasure somehow had the greatest effect on me. I wasn't sure what was going on in those pictures but it looked so appealing. The articles by the images gave context for the self-stimulation and what it accomplished.

I was learning a new vocabulary: all the words associated with sex and sensuality, words that at ten years old, I'd just never heard before. Suddenly these were words that meant something to me and they described something I began to want and desire. Even though I was just ten years old I began experimenting with what my own body could do as I looked at these pictures of other bodies. And just like that, I began my journey of struggle with pornography.

Those images made a deep impression on me even though they were just still pictures in printed magazines. But it didn't take long before I discovered VHS tapes with pornography videos. A family friend took me on a ski trip with a couple of his buddies. We crashed at his friend's place, and when they went out for the evening, I did some exploring and found these tapes. At twelve years old, the actions I was seeing were starting to make a lot more sense and to this day I cannot get the scenes out of my head. I watched those tapes until the time my family friend was supposed to return. The only saving grace was that those tapes were at a ski cabin miles away from where I lived. Otherwise, I'd have been going back to see them again and again! As I fell asleep that night I felt this mix of enticement and excitement over what I'd been watching — and guilt and shame about it at the same time.

Stories like mine are replicated by the tens of thousands all around the world. Men my age (I'm Gen-X) may have discovered pornography in a magazine they stumbled upon, but men who are millennials and Gen Z have discovered porn with far less complication, and with a far greater degree of explicit content. The advent of online videos, streaming technology, and social media have made access to pornography something that is literally two clicks away, in the palm of one's hand. According to the National Institute of Health's "Truth About Porn" article from 2020, 91.5% of American adult men, and 60.2% of American adult women admitted that they had watched porn in the last month. According to The Guardian — Thought Hub, 10% of American adults admitted to having an addiction to online pornographic material. We have a problem.

We have a problem because the internalization and consumption of pornographic material corrodes and corrupts our value for women, degrades our expectations for the beauty of wholesome sex, and desensitizes us to such an extent that 'normal sex' with our 'normal woman' wife doesn't satisfy. It causes us to waste our time, and it denigrates our sense of self-worth, because — well, 'size matters' — and now we're not sure we measure up. It causes us to become dissatisfied with our relationship with our wives because they don't 'perform' like the women we've seen online. In some instances, the use of pornography can elicit intrigue about or entry into deviant practices in the realm of LGBTQ lifestyles, polyamory, swinging, orgies, and bestiality. Pornography becomes addictive for people because it triggers the God-designed systems for arousal, stimulation, and dopamine production originally intended to serve God's original design for sex, which includes procreation, fertility, and pleasure within the proper context. Millions of men and women have become addicted to the cycle of dopamine hits that come through the use of porn — even as it does damage to anything resembling a healthy view of sex and intimacy. We have a problem.

This problem has been with us since the fall of humanity in the Garden of Eden. The problem of porn is an ancient one. In the Old Testament book of 1–2 Kings, one king after another rose up among God's people Israel. The twelve tribes were divided into North and South. God's people began adapting to the ways of the world around them, including the practice of the worship of Asherah through the use of Asherah poles, high place altars, and local shrine prostitution. The Asherah poles were something like a 'totem pole' with sexually explicit imagery carved into the wood. These were days before screens or printing presses so these carved totems were one of the de-facto ways porn was spread in that day — along with blatant idol worship of the false god Asherah. The images were given plausibility because they were supposedly about 'fertility', and isn't it just natural to desire fertility for fields and families? A few good kings were commended because they had the courage to tear down these Asherah poles and high place altars, but the vast majority of Israel's kings rebuilt them and allowed these things to flourish because it was an important element of the local economy.

Porn is also a powerful economic element in our modern day. The first porn website was established in 1994. Now, in 2023, pornography is a worldwide $100 billion industry. $12 billion of that total is from consumers of pornography in the United States. Around the world, people spend 6 billion hours, collectively, watching pornography. This does not even count the indirect economic value of the time spent on social media sites that serve as an easy funnel into explicit porn. Time and money are the essence of an economy, and many businesses that are not directly involved in porn are economically motivated to continue to create easy access to it. Add to that the growing cultural ambivalence toward the morality of porn, and you have ideal circumstances for the rapid, unchecked expansion of the pornography industry.

GOD'S MAN: TIMOTHY

Timothy is a prominent figure in the New Testament, a protege of the Apostle Paul, and he is often celebrated for his remarkable purity of character. His unwavering commitment to the teachings of Jesus Christ and his deep faith made him a shining example of moral and spiritual integrity. Timothy's purity extended not only to his personal conduct but also to his dedication to the ministry. Born to a Jewish mother and a Greek father, Timothy came to faith under Paul's ministry during one of his early missionary journeys. He quickly gained recognition for his sincere faith, dedication, and deep understanding of the Scriptures. Paul saw great potential in Timothy and chose him as a fellow laborer in spreading the teachings of Jesus Christ. This partnership with Paul allowed Timothy to play a pivotal role in the early Christian community, and he is often regarded as one of the most trusted and influential figures of his time among the followers of The Way (as Christianity was called).

Timothy was known for his genuine and selfless service to the early Christian community, which was a testament to his purity of heart and intention. Throughout his life, Timothy consistently demonstrated a life dedicated to righteousness, humility, and an unwavering pursuit of God's will, making him an enduring symbol of purity within the Christian tradition. Timothy's accomplishments were extensive and impactful. He accompanied Paul on multiple missionary journeys, serving as a key assistant and disciple. His mission work helped establish and strengthen various Christian communities in Asia Minor and Greece. Timothy was also entrusted with important tasks such as delivering Paul's letters to the churches – most notably the letters to the Corinthians, Thessalonians, and Philippians. He was made responsible as a pastor and an overseer in these places. His commitment to the faith, his leadership skills, and his ability to communicate effectively made him a crucial link in the spread of Christianity throughout the ancient world. As a result, Timothy's legacy endures as a symbol of dedicated service and loyalty to the early Christian movement. The purity of his character became a multiplier of his impact for the glory of God! As Christian men, Timothy's life can be an example to us. If you have the time, read through the books of the Bible that bear his name: 1 and 2 Timothy. They are written by Paul — to Timothy — but from these words you will discover the kind of man Timothy was based on what Paul entrusted him to do and teach. If you have more time, read 2 Corinthians as well. The text indicates that Timothy was co-author of that book (and Philippians, Philemon, Thessalonians, and Colossians!), along with Paul. Reference the passages below as you dig deeper.

DIGGING DEEPER: TIMOTHY

1   **Read Acts 16:1–5 and 1 Corinthians 4:17.** What is the correlation between Timothy's reputation and further opportunity for him in serving God? What factors do you think may have led to people's positive view of him?

2   **Read Philippians 2:19–23.** What was it about Timothy that was so remarkable? While this passage is not about pornography, think it through: What does this passage reveal about the way Timothy lived in purity? And what could that mean for you in your pursuit of purity?

3   **Read 2 Corinthians 1:19.** How did Timothy's 'yes' empower his life for Jesus? How does a 'yes' carry power? How could a 'yes' in Jesus empower you to overcome pornography — as opposed to simply 'no'?

4   **Read 1 Timothy 4:12.** Why was it important that Timothy consider his personal example as a leader? Why does something 'private' like purity matter in someone's leadership? How does your example in all things, including purity, affect or connect with your example and leadership?

5   **Read 1 Timothy 5:1–2.** These words from Paul to Timothy gave him a standard to live up to. Do you accept this standard? If you are viewing porn, are you keeping this standard?

YOUR KINGDOM ASSIGNMENT:
RISE UP WITH AN EYE RIPPED OUT (PURITY)

I know the heading sounds extreme, but sometimes our actions have to be extreme when the problem is severe. The problem of pornography is catastrophic, and we serve a Savior who died on the cross to set us free from the penalty of sin, and who gave us the capacity to live above the power of sin. Exercising the capacity to live above sin's power is not a spiritual magic trick of some kind. We don't get let off the hook with some superficial spiritual bypassing. Our Savior spoke words calling for severe action against sinful tendencies when He said:

"If your right eye causes you to stumble, gouge it out and throw it away. It is better for you to lose one part of your body than for your whole body to be thrown into hell." Matthew 2:29 NIV

Just in case you're the kind of guy who thinks every single thing in the Bible should be taken literally, let me introduce you to the concept of hyperbole (high-PER-bowl-ee), which is metaphorical language that raises the stakes in order to grip your attention and enforce the seriousness and importance of something. Jesus is not literally expecting to have a mass number of one-eyed disciples running around the world. But He is calling for us as His disciples to be ruthless and strong in our actions when it comes to sin. He is calling us to be men who will be willing to take bold, even costly action to root out, diminish, and disallow the power of sin to corrupt us! With regard to pornography, there are some eyeballs that need to be ripped out — figuratively speaking. What I'm talking about is taking bold action to do what we can to eradicate sinful patterns and to put measures in place that will make it more difficult for us to step into sin. This may look like deleting social media, or creating a household rule that includes you which says 'no computer use behind closed doors', or it may look like giving your wife total access to your phone and passwords so she can spot-check your history at any moment, or using a location tracking app where your buddy — or your wife — can see your location at all times. These are some examples of practical steps you may need to take. At the same time, a more comprehensive process is in order. Because you are serious about kicking porn, let me give it to you straight. In short, here's how to tear out your eye: repent, renounce, rewire, and regroup.

1. REPENT OF THE SIN OF WATCHING PORN AND MASTURBATING!

"Repent, then, and turn to God, so that your sins may be wiped out, that times of refreshing may come from the Lord, and that he may send the Messiah, who has been appointed for you—even Jesus." Acts 3:19–20

You need to realize that indulging in watching porn, or indulging in watching porn and masturbating are both sinful. If you continue to sin, you will stay in the shadows, and you may lose the strength of your connection with God. Broadly speaking, porn falls under the Biblical category of sexual immorality. God's Word says, "Flee from sexual immorality. All other sins a person commits are outside the body, but whoever sins sexually, sins against their own body." (1 Corinthians 6:18 NIV) God's word calls sexual immorality sin — and when we have sinned, we must repent. Don't just say. "God I'm sorry I looked at porn." Come into His Holy presence, and say:

"Father, forgive me, I stepped in a dirty pile of sin by looking at that porn. I sinned against you. It is wrong, it is sin, and I repent! I thought it would satisfy me, I thought it would be fine — but I violated what Your Word says! I repent — I change my thinking right now — and I accept Your thoughts God — that sexual immorality is wrong and I repent; forgive me God for that sin!"

We can easily become desensitized to the reality of sin; repentance helps us to recalibrate around what is right and what is wrong, and more importantly, around who gets to say what's right or wrong! So step one of ripping out your eye is to repent. Don't dance around it, saying, "Oh I tripped up a little." Don't sugar coat it, saying, "Okay, I might have had a little struggle." Admit that sin for what it is. Repent of it. God's promise from Acts 3:19–20 is that as you do the repenting, He does the removing and the refreshing! Don't you want that? Even if you have to do this every other day as you're first getting free, do it. Repent of the sin of watching porn and masturbating!

2. RENOUNCE THE UNINTENTIONAL PARTNERSHIP YOU ENGAGED IN WITH THE DEMONIC REALM THROUGH PORN!

"So put to death the sinful, earthly things lurking within you. Have nothing to do with sexual immorality, impurity, lust, and evil desires."
Colossians 3:5

In the vision of Heaven and the Last Things that is portrayed in the book of Revelation, there is a depiction of Babylon as a spiritual entity — and what this spiritual entity has done in the world is exposed. In Revelation 14:1 it says, "A second angel followed and said, "'Fallen! Fallen is Babylon the Great,' which made all the nations drink the maddening wine of her adulteries." While this scripture has a specific context related to the last days and the second coming, it also gives us a look behind the veil in the spiritual realm. What we find is that the temptation to sin — specifically in sexual immorality and lust — is brought about by sinister demonic forces. The implication is that when we do decide to indulge in pornography, we are inadvertently partnering with the demonic realm. Once we have repented of our sin in this regard, the next thing we need to do is to renounce 'the deal we made with the devil' so to speak. Here's what that looks like: after your prayer of repentance, you say,

"In the mighty Name of Jesus, I renounce every evil spirit that I unintentionally partnered with by engaging in pornography! I declare the blood of Jesus over my mind, body, soul, and spirit, cleansing me from any demonic entanglements from this!"

We must remain in our freedom in Christ and refuse to allow the schemes of the devil to dislodge us from that freedom. If we've sinned and in particular, partnered with the demonic realm — even unintentionally — those powers may claim some right to afflict or oppress us further. These matters remain somewhat mysterious, even in the pages of the scriptures. But the idea from Ephesians 6:11 is that the armor of God is to be put on, not just so you can stand around in it, but so that in it you can take your stand against the devil's schemes — and pornography falls under that category. So renounce the evil spirits behind porn and renounce your partnership with them that came about through your engagement with porn!

3. REWIRE YOUR BRAIN TO MOVE INTO PURITY OUT OF A DEEPER PURSUIT OF GOD!

"It is God's will that you should be sanctified: that you should avoid sexual immorality; that each of you should learn to control your own body in a way that is holy and honorable, not in passionate lust like the pagans, who do not know God; and that in this matter no one should wrong or take advantage of a brother or sister. The Lord will punish all those who commit such sins, as we told you and warned you before. For God did not call us to be impure, but to live a holy life. Therefore, anyone who rejects this instruction does not reject a human being but God, the very God who gives you his Holy Spirit." 1 Thessalonians 4:3–8 NIV

You have physical impulses, you have desires, and you have inclinations. We all do. And we all learn to restrain our impulses, at least in polite company, and that is good. But God is calling you to be the kind of man who will also do this in private. In the passage from 1 Thessalonians above, there are several operative verbs: "avoid" and "learn," to be exact. Yes, God says point blank 'avoid sexual immorality' and that includes porn. Did you know that in the original Greek text of this verse, the word for 'sexual immorality' is one Greek word: πορνεία — or, transliterated, pornea. Yes, we get our word pornography from this Greek root word. Could the scriptures be any more clear? Avoid porn, says the Lord! Avoid porn along with any and every other illicit sexual action.

You need to rewire your brain. The passage above calls for us to learn to control our bodies in ways that are holy and honorable. If you had to list out 15 things you could do with your body right now that are holy and honorable, could you? I bet you could. And you should because those are the very things that you need to rewire your brain to opt for when you face the temptation to sin with porn.

You need to rewire your brain to seek out satisfaction, pleasure, and intimacy in relationship with God. If you are going to stay in a place of purity, you simply cannot indulge your sexual appetite in whatever way you desire. On one hand, that could feel like nothing but deprivation; on the other hand, you have an opportunity to rewire your brain to pursue fulfillment in God and in His gifts of creativity, athleticism, sport, adventure, craftsmanship, productivity, entertainment, and music. While this may require a 'no' to the fulfillment of a specific sexual desire, that does not mean you will not have fulfillment! It may help you to state out loud, as a personal declaration:

"I will find fulfillment and satisfaction in as many godly ways as possible. I will be satisfied and fulfilled in and through my connection with Christ!"

As you rewire your brain and move into purity through a deeper pursuit of God, you will find alternate means to satisfaction. There are replacements that God will allow you to discover that will create a sense of gratitude and excitement for you. You'll need to acknowledge that currently, there are circuits in your brain that are used to convey the current of hormonal arousal and desire into one place and one place only — porn and masturbation. Acknowledge that faulty wiring for what it is and defy the lie that there is only one way for you to experience satisfaction and fulfillment. Step up your faith and your pursuit of God and discover just how powerful God is — that He is even capable of giving you the deepest sense of fulfillment, connection, closeness, and even pleasure that you can imagine. It's a holy pleasure, a holy goodness, that has the strength to override and rewire your brain's current default setting of addiction!

4. REGROUP WITH OTHER BELIEVERS WHO ALSO WANT TO WIN AGAINST PORN!
"Therefore confess your sins to each other and pray for each other so that you may be healed. The prayer of a righteous person is powerful and effective." James 5:16 NIV

When Jesus created the Body we know as The Church, His vision was less about a magnificent institution with impressive buildings (although those facilities and organizations are useful, and can be used for His glory!), and more about a movement of people who are being transformed from the inside out by the Spirit of God. As He walked the dusty pathways of the Middle East, He rose in indignation against the pharisaical religious leaders of his day because they were not actually living a transformed life, but a superficial life based on mere religious appearances. He railed against them, saying, "Woe to you, Pharisees!" because of their hypocrisy. He wanted people to come into a true community of like-mindedness about earnestly seeking God — and truly seeking to live God's way — not play pretend with religious themes!

MAN ARISE AS A MAN FREE FROM PORNOGRAPHY

To step into the authentic community Jesus had in mind, you need to regroup with people who are also willing to do just that. Even though the statistics on porn use are extremely alarming, not every guy in church is ready to 'go there' in transparent community. You need to find the ones who are. Whether through your church, through a recovery group, through accountability partnerships, or through RUK, you need to find men with whom you can confess your sin — point blank — without mincing words. You need to find those men who can look you in the eye and remind you of the power you have to overcome. You need to get with a group of men who are determined to hold each other up and prod each other toward greater and greater freedom from sexual sin and the use of porn.

As you do regroup with other believers who want to win against porn, you should give one another the space to confess sin. But also, you should leave room for intentional prayer; the promise is not just that we confess our sins, but that we pray for each other boldly and full of faith — for breakthrough! Even as I write this, my wife is out of town for the weekend and I am home alone. Normally that would be a huge danger zone for me. But I can literally hear the words of my accountability partner, Brett, as he prayed for me in the parking lot of the coffee shop where we meet on Thursday mornings: "Oh God, give John victory this weekend when Ann is out of town! Help him overcome every temptation and stay in the place of purity!" God heard his prayers. So did I. God is responding in the spiritual realm to his fervent prayer for me. But you know what else is happening? I'm remembering his prayers even as I face moments of possibility where I could step in a pile of sin. Recalling the 'fervent prayers of a righteous person' who knew what I'd be facing motivates me, pushes me, provokes me, and calls me to a kind of holy sobriety and a desire to stay there!

THE REST OF JOHN'S STORY

As Christian men, we recognize that pornography is sinful. But think about what that means: when we indulge in watching pornography, we are practicing outright disobedience to God. When we watch porn, we are dishonoring our Father in Heaven and trampling underfoot the beauty and goodness of the costly grace provided by the shed blood of the Lord Jesus Christ. When we view porn, we are resisting and possibly quenching the Holy Spirit of the Living God. Further, we have to recognize that pornography is demonic in and of itself; use of it opens the door to demonic affliction and oppression in our lives and in our families. It is a portal to hell itself and we blithely open it with two or three thumb swipes across a screen or a click or two on a mouse. We have a problem.

We have a problem, but we also have a solution. The solution is in Jesus Christ himself. A couple of years ago at a men's retreat for our church, there was a time for testimonies. I will never forget the moment a man named JC stood and shared his own. A man in his 50's, he stood and said, "My testimony is that I have not looked at porn or masturbated in 527 days!" I was shocked because of the boldness of his declaration and the freedom from shame with which he made it. I was also shocked because even though I was speaking at that men's retreat, I was pretty sure I couldn't have personally made that declaration. Even though my actions on both of those fronts were minimal, it wasn't total victory like this brother had. He learned to walk in victory by surrounding himself with other brothers who were willing and ready to get real about this very serious problem. This group of men determined together to walk in the resurrection power of Jesus Christ in overcoming the demonic stronghold and physical addiction to pornography!

I want to challenge you to believe it is truly possible for you to get free from pornography addiction and use. It's possible to live in purity! This chapter has shown you, in an abbreviated way, a pathway that will allow you to come into the light and break the bondage of pornography off your life. What I have shared here is my own approach to living in freedom from pornography use, because I want to have a testimony like JC's that one day moves beyond a number of days in freedom, to a number of years in freedom, and then to a number of decades in freedom! There are thousands of books on the topic and one chapter in this Bible study shouldn't take the place of the deeper dive you may need to do in your journey to freedom. At the end of this chapter, I will list several helpful resources that you may want to grab hold of to process this crucial aspect of spiritual life more thoroughly.

KINGS DISCUSSION QUESTIONS

1   If you got a phone call from a group doing an anonymous study on porn use — and your name would not be shared — how would you answer this question: Have you viewed pornography at all in the last 30 days?

What are the things that trigger you to want to give in to looking at porn and/or masturbating? What step could you take to address or eliminate that trigger?

2   **Read Ephesians 5:3–5 and describe how these words motivate you to desire to abstain from porn and live in sexual purity.** What do you observe about people who have not heeded these words?? How does that motivate you?

When was the last time you indulged in masturbation — and what were the conditions that led to it? What specific kind of porn access point did you use — website, app, etc.? What steps did you take after the act? Did you try to cover up your steps?

3   **Read Mathew 5:28 and 1 Corinthians 6:9–11.** How do Jesus' words convict you with regard to lust? How do you think He feels about the women in the porn videos you've watched? How does it affect you to reflect on what Jesus did for you to make you different than you used to be without Him?

How would you feel if it were your daughter in the video and you observed some man satisfying himself while watching her? Yeah — I'm trying to make you lose your appetite!

ARISE AND ACCEPT THE CHALLENGE

1   Delete the app that is the source of the greatest temptation and easiest access for porn for you.

2   Ask a brother to be an accountability partner to you. Tell him your goal is to walk in greater purity.

3   Go sign up for an SA or sexual purity ministry group in your church or through RUK!

4   Delete your hidden secret browser from your phone!

ADDITIONAL RESOURCES:

Every Man's Battle by Stephen Arterburn

No More Excuses by Tony Evans

The Purity Principle by Randy Alcorn

Pure Desire by Ted Roberts

www.puredesire.org

https://earthweb.com/how-much-is-the-porn-industry-worth/

A MAN WHO IS A WARRIOR

"When you go out to fight your enemies and you face horses and chariots and an army greater than your own, do not be afraid. The Lord your God, who brought you out of the land of Egypt, is with you!"

Deuteronomy 20:1, NLT

JOHN'S STORY: WAKING UP TO WARRIOR STATUS

My neighbor across the street, Chris, is an Army veteran. He fought in Afghanistan on behalf of our country and now has a new career as an entrepreneur. He is a private and corporate chef. He is a compassionate and kind guy. One day a couple years ago, Chris came over and gave me a whole smoked trout he'd made. It was the best fish I'd had in my life! He's a thoughtful and generous guy. But he's also a warrior at heart.

Last year, he put a flag up over his garage, stating, "LIONS, NOT SHEEP!" This sentiment has arisen over the last couple years and many of us embrace it. We recognize that spiritually, we are "sheep" who know the Lord as our shepherd. But in this life, in this world, we see a need for men of God to rise up and take a stand — to be lions, not sheep.

Brother, it is time for your roar to be heard, for your fighting strength to be increased and demonstrated. It is time for you to take your place on the battleground — to rise up with a warrior spirit for the Glory of God — like Joshua did. Let's explore more about God's man Joshua.

GOD'S MAN: JOSHUA

Joshua was a significant figure in the Bible, known for his courage, faith, and leadership. He was born as a slave in Egypt and later became a trusted aide to, and general for, Moses. After Moses' death, Joshua became the leader of the Israelites and led them in their conquest of the Promised Land in the 1200's BC. He is remembered for his unwavering faith in God, his boldness in battle, and his commitment to following God's commands. Joshua's name means "the Lord is salvation," and his life story serves as an inspiration for godly men to trust in God, have courage in the face of adversity, and to fight for the things that God has spoken and promised. Joshua's story in the Bible matters because it shows us what it means to be a man who lives out his faith with courage and strength. Joshua's leadership skills and military tactics serve as valuable lessons for those of us in positions of authority. Overall, Joshua's story is a testament to the power of courage based in faith and the strength that comes from following God's will. Read the whole book of Joshua if you can, but at least review and refer to the passages below as you dig deeper.

DIGGING DEEPER: JOSHUA

1   **Read Exodus 17:9–14 and Joshua 1:1–9.** God commands Joshua to be strong and courageous as he leads the Israelites into the Promised Land. What can you learn from Joshua's example of courage and faith in following God's commands? How can you apply this example to your own life as a Christian man?

2   **Read Joshua 3:1–17.** How did Joshua provide spiritual leadership to his people? What did he ask them to do (in verses 5 and 9), and what effect did his request have? How did Joshua establish his military strategy, and how did it work out? What does the miraculous crossing of the Jordan reveal to you about what is possible?

3   **Read Joshua 4:1–24.** What was Joshua's relationship with God like? How do you think he actually received the revelation God was giving him? How did Joshua combine both tactical planning and spiritual insight?

4   **Read Joshua 6.** What can you learn from the Israelites' obedience to God, even when His commands may seem unusual or difficult to understand? Describe Joshua's leadership in this episode. How can you cultivate a deeper faith and a willingness to obey God in your own life and provide courageous leadership like He did?

5   **Read Joshua 8:1–29.** What lessons can we learn about strategy and leadership from Joshua's battle plan for Ai? How can we apply these principles to our own lives and the challenges we face?

YOUR KINGDOM ASSIGNMENT: BECOME COURAGEOUS!

By now, you're getting a clearer picture of the kind of courage God wants to draw out from within you. You're getting a stronger sense of what a courageous man with a warrior spirit looks like as you read the scriptures. God has made you unique, with your own capacity, gifts, talents, and abilities — and His desire is that you would be fortified with courage rooted in your trust in God's character. He wants you to be a warrior in this world for what is right; a warrior on behalf of your family; a warrior on behalf of your marriage; a warrior for the enterprise He's called you to lead; a warrior for God's Kingdom! It's time to step up in God's assignment on your life and roar! Here are four core actions you need to take to do just that.

1. TAKE TIME TO DEEPEN YOUR FAITH!

"But grow in the grace and knowledge of our Lord and Savior Jesus Christ." 2 Peter 3:18 NIV

Your capacity for courage will be increased by your time in God's presence. God is the source of all of your strength, energy, vitality, and ultimate victory. Be a man who is close to God and you'll never be far from the origin and fountain of triumph! Spend time in prayer, read and study God's word, and seek a deeper relationship with Him. By deepening your faith, you will be better equipped to face the challenges of life with courage and conviction.

2. TAKE YOUR PLACE AMONG YOUR BROTHERS IN THE BODY!

"Now you are the body of Christ, and each one of you is a part of it." 1 Corinthians 12:27 NIV

Can you imagine an army winning a war if each soldier just went off alone and tried to engage in the fight by themselves? Even our most elite fighting forces deploy in teams or squads of 5–10, within larger units. It was God's plan to establish groups of Christian believers, called churches, all around the world. You are meant to take your place in the Body of Christ among your fellow brothers who are believers! Iron sharpens iron. Be an active member of your church community, and build meaningful relationships with other believers! When you find and give that support and encouragement, the ability to engage in the fight is elevated!

3. TAKE ACTION THAT IS BOLD!

"The wicked flee though no one pursues, but the righteous are as bold as a lion." Proverbs 28:1 NIV

Brother — you are meant to be one who takes initiative! Step out of your comfort zone, take risks, and pursue your goals with boldness and determination. As Joshua 1:9 says, "Be strong and courageous. Do not be afraid; do not be discouraged, for the Lord your God will be with you wherever you go." Your community needs you to show up. Your business needs you to start roaring with something new that breaks the inertia. Be bold, and take action! Resist passivity!

4. TAKE YOUR STAND AGAINST THE DEVIL!

"Submit yourselves, then, to God. Resist the devil, and he will flee from you." James 4:7 NIV

You've got to recognize that we are engaged in a spiritual battle. Do what God's Word says! Stand firm in your faith, and resist the lies and temptations of the enemy. Read through Ephesians 6:1–18 and discover what a fully armed believer looks like. Tear down demonic strongholds in thought and life patterns. Stop cooperating with the devil by being in your flesh and get in the Spirit! Take authority through the Blood of Christ over your family, your business, and your community. Cast out demons like your mighty Savior Jesus did!

In summary, as a Christian man, you can take time to deepen your faith, take your place among your brothers in the Body, take bold action, and take your stand against the devil. By taking these actions, you will be well on your way to living a life of courage, roaring with passion and a warrior spirit that honors God and makes a positive impact in the world.

MAN ARISE AS A WARRIOR

God's design for you, man of God, is that you'd rise up with courage and the spirit of a warrior! The Bible is replete with passages detailing the warrior spirit of godly men. Think of Joshua who led the Hebrew nation into the promised land with one great war victory after another, Gideon who led the 300 to great victory, David who slayed Goliath, and Elijah who outright slaughtered the 400 prophets of Baal on Mount Carmel. Because of the faith and courage of these men of God who had a warrior spirit about them, families were protected, wives were blessed, homes were made strong, cities were established and improved, evil was defeated, and a nation prospered!

Brother, it is my conviction that you YOU are meant to be such a man as these! Our battle is not against a pagan nation, but we do have a battle to fight, and it takes place on many fronts. We have conflict against apathy, complacency, and laziness. We have swords drawn against sin and unrighteousness in our own lives. We are fighting for prosperity and goodness in our businesses and enterprises and civic pursuits. We are at war in the spiritual realm with the devil himself who comes to kill, steal and destroy.

THE REST OF JOHN'S STORY

Men of courage must not simply accept whatever fodder the big media empires are providing; we must not just go along to get along with whatever the spirit of the age is pushing for; we must not quietly acquiesce to whatever our culture says is now acceptable. No, this is a time when the roar of the lion must be heard.

My neighbor put up that flag because he was waking up to warrior status. He recognized that passivity would serve no one. I want to be a lion, not a sheep! What about you? How do you feel about the direction things seem to be headed? Will you remain passive and just shuffle along with the direction that's been established? Or would you join me and be willing to recognize there is something that sets you apart: Christ in you, the hope of glory! He's the Lamb of God — yes — but he is also the Lion of Judah, and He lives in you!

⛨ KINGS DISCUSSION QUESTIONS

1   On a scale of 1–10, rate how well you're living as a courageous warrior, and give a recent example of why or how.

⛨ *Which of the four elements of your kingdom assignment actions of being a warrior kind of sucks right now? What are you willing to do about it?*

2   **Read 1 Corinthians 16:13–14.** How can we balance the qualities of courage and love in our interactions with our families, coworkers, and communities?

That passage listed five key actions for a man of God with a warrior spirit. Pick one that you are not living up to and decide what needs to change. State some examples of actions you could take, and then let your brothers hold you accountable.

3   **Read Deuteronomy 20:1 and Psalm 18:39.** What can you do to apply this same faith and confidence to your personal and professional battles today?

What has recently caused your confidence to take a hit?

4   **Read Ecclesiastes 3:8 and Psalm 144:1.** How can we discern when it is appropriate to fight for what we believe in, and when we should seek a more peaceful resolution to our conflicts? How can we move towards becoming effective warriors for our families, businesses, and communities?

5   **Read Proverbs 28:1 and Hebrews 11:1.** What kind of bold step of faith do you sense God calling you to make?

Name the comforts and securities that you are clinging to that feel more important to you than the bold faith move God may be calling you to make. Then repent!

6   **Read Ephesians 6:1–18.** Why is the armor of God important, and what is your process for putting it on? What does it actually look like for you to engage in spiritual warfare? Is there a way that your spiritual warfare needs to take place in the natural realm?

Which of the defensive weapons are you not putting on well?

ARISE AND ACCEPT THE CHALLENGE

1 Look up that old Twisted Sister song, 'We're Not Gonna Take It!' Blast it, and think of ten things that are on your 'not gonna take it' list — in your own life, your own mind, your community, your business. Write 'em down, and pin 'em up!

2 Get together with a godly brother and do a 'crazy goals' duel: put out an actual, realistic goal in any area of life, one at a time. The brother needs to one-up you on that same topic, with another actual achievable goal that's a little more ballsy than yours. Repeat, as long as you can, then pray in boldness for each other to hit some of those goals!

3 March around your house and in every room, take authority over the space. In every room, say: 'I take authority over this room; I cast out any evil or unclean Spirit, in Jesus' Name!'

4 Do a prayer walk of spiritual authority around your community, your children's school, or a government building with at least one other Christian brother. As you walk, pray for God's blessing over the place, and cast out or tear down anything demonic.

A MAN OF ENDURANCE

"Therefore, since we are surrounded by such a huge crowd of witnesses to the life of faith, let us strip off every weight that slows us down, especially the sin that so easily trips us up. And let us run with endurance the race God has set before us."

Hebrews 12:1, NLT

JOHN'S STORY: THE DIGNITY OF ENDURANCE

Several years ago, I had some friends who came back all excited after a weekend adventure called 'the Ragnar.' I asked, "What's a Ragnar?" My buddy Doug explained that Ragnar is the name of one of the great Viking kings, famous for uniting the Scandinavian Viking clans in pursuit of conquering distant lands like England. After the history lesson, he went on to say that it was also the name of a nearly 200-mile 24-hour team relay race that he and five others had just completed. He and another guy said I HAD to do it with them the next year, and even though I hadn't run more than half a mile at any one time since my college days, I said yes.

Four months before the Ragnar race, the guys said it was time to start training. Because of everyone's work schedules, we had to meet at 4:30 am to do our running. The guys agreed that since I was new to running, they'd pull me along and start me off easy. The goal was to get me from running half a mile in one day up to running 30 miles in one day over the course of four months of training. The first day we met to run, it was 50 degrees outside. We ran with headlamps strapped around our brows and the run was a doable out-and-back totalling 1.5 miles. The next morning we ran again, and they pushed me to complete four miles. This felt like a major accomplishment to me and I was proud that I'd made it.

The next day, it was time to run again, but when I woke up, my legs shook as I descended the stairs. My feet hurt, and my shins were in pain. I looked out the window. It was raining, and it was 35 degrees. Nobody runs in weather like that! I texted Doug and said, "I don't think I can make it." He shot back, "Come on man, don't wuss out on us!" I went, and it was miserable. I'm telling you it was terrible! I ran with resentment in every step: why did I have to do this? What was this about? My legs were shaking. It was wet and cold and I was deeply irritated to be doing this. But you know what? I completed a five-mile run that morning because some brothers pushed me past my comfort zone and into the endurance zone.

Later that day, Itold at least ten people about the run I'd done that morning. I mentioned it casually, "Yeah, on my five-mile run this morning, I went right past your neighborhood!" I relished the impressed looks. "You ran today? In the 30 degrees and the rain?" "Yeah, of course!" Little did they know I'd never done that before in my life!

There are many examples of endurance in the Bible. Hebrews 11 lists countless people whose endurance landed the memory of their life in the 'hall of faith' in the Bible. From the Old Testament to the New, endurance is praised and empowered by God. Consider Job, who lost it all and pushed forward anyway. Remember Gideon, who fought to victory against thousands with just 300 of his own men. In the New Testament, there is one man whose endurance led to an explosion of new life and faith in Christ across the globe. That man is the Apostle Paul.

GOD'S MAN: THE APOSTLE PAUL

The Apostle Paul was a prominent figure in the early Christian Church. He was born under the name Saul in Tarsus (present-day Turkey) in the first century AD. Paul was originally a zealous opponent of Christianity, and he persecuted the followers of Jesus until he experienced a dramatic conversion on the road to Damascus. After his conversion, Paul became one of the most important leaders of the early Christian movement, and he wrote many of the books of the New Testament. Paul faced many challenges and hardships during his ministry. He faced opposition from those who rejected his teachings, including Jewish leaders and pagan authorities. He endured beatings, imprisonment, and shipwrecks, but he remained steadfast in his faith and continued to spread the message of Christ throughout the Mediterranean world. He is known for his missionary journeys, during which he established many Christian communities and churches. Paul's teachings emphasized the importance of faith in Jesus Christ, salvation through grace, and the unity of all believers in Christ. His legacy continues to influence Christian theology and practice to this day. Inspired by the Holy Spirit, Paul wrote nearly half of the New Testament books, including Romans, 1–2 Corinthians, Philippians, Galatians, 1–2 Thessalonians, 1–2 Timothy, and more. The narrative of Paul's early journeys is recorded in the second half of the book of Acts.

DIGGING DEEPER: PAUL

1 **Read Acts 9:1–19.** What do you think motivated Paul to persecute Christians? What were some of the elements of his conversion experience? What does that say to you about what it may take for someone to come to Christ?

2 **Read Acts 13:50–51, Acts 14:19–20, 2 Corinthians 11:23–28, & Acts 16:22–24 and Philippians 1:12–17.** Describe how you would feel if you endured some of the difficulties that Paul did. What gave him the strength to keep going?

3 **Read Acts 27:13–44.** Describe the elements of leadership and character you see in Paul through this crisis. How did Paul bring encouragement and strength in the midst of the challenge?

4 **Read 2 Corinthians 11:23–33, Philippians 3:3–7.** What motivated Paul to endure so much hardship? How did Paul's experience of suffering empower, equip, and ultimately strengthen him?

5   **Read Philippians 1:12–26 and 2 Timothy 4:6–8.** How did perspective play a role in Paul's perseverance? What are some adjectives you would use to describe Paul?

YOUR KINGDOM ASSIGNMENT: RISE UP AS A MAN OF ENDURANCE

In life, we are faced with many challenges and obstacles that can test our faith and resilience. However, as a follower of Christ, you have access to a prevailing strength that can carry you through them all: the power of the resurrection of Jesus Christ. His victory makes it possible for you to endure and persevere through all of life's trials and opportunities. This endurance requires a certain level of GRIT — a combination of four key factors that you must choose and cultivate in your life. As you do, the resurrection power of Christ will carry you along with each step you take. The acrostic GRIT will introduce you to the biblical foundations of your kingdom assignment.

G – GO AND GET IT!

"Go to the ant, you sluggard; consider its ways and be wise! It has no commander, no overseer or ruler, yet it stores its provisions in summer and gathers its food at harvest." Proverbs 6:6–8 NIV

The first factor of GRIT is the drive to go and get it! As a man of endurance, you recognize that your pursuits still matter, even while you're dealing with hard things! So, build up a resolve inside of yourself. Even when you're facing struggles in your marriage or pressures in your business, you still keep going after it! In marriage, it's love, romance, and healthy connection you want. So go and get it! With your business and your work, it's profitability and provision you want. So go and get it! Take the action that needs to be taken. Decide here and now that you will not let the hard things grind the 'get it!' out of you! There's an old Latin saying my grandfather shared with me: illigitimus non carbarundum: don't let the bastards grind you down! Those were his words, not mine! Not sure if we should put that in a Bible study, but we just did!

R – RESILIENCE

"The godly may trip seven times, but they will get up again. But one disaster is enough to overthrow the wicked." Proverbs 24:16, NLT

"Dear brothers and sisters, when troubles of any kind come your way, consider it an opportunity for great joy. For you know that when your faith is tested, your endurance has a chance to grow. So let it grow, for when your endurance is fully developed, you will be perfect and complete, needing nothing." James 1:2–4 NLT

The second factor of GRIT is Resilience. Resilience means having the mental and emotional toughness to withstand adversity and keep pressing forward. My brother, things are going to get tough, and they might even knock you down. Get back up and keep going. Disappointment and problems may blindside you, and knock you out like a left hook straight out of hell. Get up, shake off the dust, and keep going. Sing Chumbawamba to yourself: "I get knocked down, but I get up again. You're never gonna keep me down!" Take time to grieve and mourn the losses, but keep in mind that endurance is all about continued momentum. You must remember that God has given you a spirit of power, love, and self-discipline, and you can call on Him for strength in times of weakness (2 Timothy 1:7). You can also take heart in the fact that Jesus has overcome the world, securing victory over death, hell, and the grave! So cultivate that resilient spirit. You'll find the more times you get back up and keep on going, the stronger you'll be at doing just that!

I – INSPIRATION

"But one thing I do: Forgetting what is behind and straining toward what is ahead, I press on toward the goal to win the prize for which God has called me heavenward in Christ Jesus." Philippians 3:13–14 NIV

The third factor of GRIT is Inspiration. In order to push through the trials and tribulations of life, you need to keep your 'why' in front of you. What is your reason for living? That source of inspiration is the fuel for the motor that can keep you moving through the mud. Perhaps your inspiration is the eternal reward in heaven promised in Philippians 3:14. Your inspiration may also be something much closer: your wife, your marriage, your children, your siblings, or the legacy you want to pass on. Identify your 'why' and let it be your inspiration in those moments when you're tempted to quit!

T – TENACITY

"We do this by keeping our eyes on Jesus, the champion who initiates and perfects our faith. Because of the joy awaiting him, he endured the cross, disregarding its shame. Now he is seated in the place of honor beside God's throne. Think of all the hostility he endured from sinful people; then you won't become weary and give up." Hebrews 12:2–3 NLT

The fourth factor of GRIT is Tenacity. Tenacity means having a never-give-up attitude and a willingness to keep pushing forward, no matter how difficult the journey may be. Sometimes, in order to be tenacious, you've got to surrender the pain you're feeling and the worries you're carrying directly to Jesus. Ask Him to lift the burden from you and to give you strength to keep going. You have to remember that God is with you, and He will never leave you or forsake you (Deuteronomy 31:6). Brother, when you face a setback, engage your faith, and reframe it. That setback is a setup for your next step up! Envision yourself like a bulldog: you get your bite on something and you don't let go! You anticipate that God is still going to show His faithfulness to you, and you get up and keep going!

Brother, choose to cultivate GRIT in your life. Decide that this is the kind of man you are: a man of grit with mental and emotional toughness. You are a man who will 'go and get it'. You're a man who is resilient. You're a man who knows his Inspiration and has the tenacity to get back up and keep fighting the good fight of the faith!

MAN ARISE AS A MAN OF ENDURANCE

Those brutal training runs reminded me of Jesus' promise that in this life we will have troubles. It should never surprise us that there are so many. We've been given fair warning! Rather than resent the trials and difficulties, embrace them! They are the very things that will test your mettle and deepen your strength. We can pray for trials and troubles to end and sometimes, God will do that for us. But until he does, the troubles, problems, and pain can serve God's purpose and strengthen us. In this life, the trial is the treasure, the obstacle is the way, and the pain is the path.

Right now, the world needs men who have grit about them, who are willing to engage in this life with endurance and do the hard things that create value and stability. We are living in difficult days and these are times in which godly men must resist the urge to quit. There is too much at stake, too much to lose, and so much to gain. The world needs you, brother, to rise up as a man who has that winner's edge, the capacity to run with endurance in this life!

THE REST OF JOHN'S STORY

After that five-mile run in the cold rain, I continued to train for the Ragnar. Four months later, I was in the van with six others running the Ragnar relay race. I personally completed nearly 30 miles in one 24-hour period in three legs. Now THAT was truly an accomplishment!

Running that Ragnar race was a blast, and it was a pretty intense physical experience. I was truly proud of the accomplishment, and the word that summarizes the entire experience for me is endurance. My buddies pushed me to the limits of my endurance as we trained. And during the actual race, when I wanted to quit, it was grit — trained into me by that team — that kept me in stride.

Brother, there are so many good things that God has for you in this life — feats, achievements, accomplishments — but to reach any of them, you will need to be a man who perseveres under pressure. Your ability to keep grinding when other people are getting lazy is what will set you apart and lift you up. The degree of success and victory you achieve in this life will be directly correlated to the capacity to endure that you've developed. Endurance. This is what separates the men from the boys. Brother, I want you to be a man of endurance! There is so much dignity in being a man who does not throw in the towel, who does not back down when it gets difficult, who does not walk away because of the harsh weather. I want you to be that kind of man, who can take on the trials and troubles with a spirit of strength and boldness!

KINGS DISCUSSION QUESTIONS

1   Name some of the things you've had to endure in your life.

Give yourself a grade on your grit — on the whole, how much grit do you think you exhibit when you face challenges?

2   **Read Colossians 3:23–24 and Proverbs 6:6–8.** Share about some moments in your life when you took initiative, took action, and made something happen. What motivated you?

Describe why it's been so long since you've taken initiative on something important — and where you sense God calling you to 'get up and go for it'.

3   **Read Philippians 3:13–15, 2 Corinthians 4:8–9, and James 1:2–4,12.** If you were to apply these verses to your own life, what do you hear the scriptures calling you to? ?

Talk about something that has kicked your butt recently. What is it going to take for you to be resilient in this moment?

4   **Read Hebrews 12:2–4.** What was the inspiration for Jesus to keep moving forward? How are you moved by the example of Jesus?

Describe what will happen to your legacy, your marriage, and your children if you give up, back down, and walk away in the face of adversity.

5   **Read 1 Corinthians 15:58 and Psalm 18:28–29.** What do these verses indicate about the kind of tenacity men of God are made for? What kind of experiences of tenacity like this have you had?

Where do you need to show some tenacity in your life right now?

ARISE AND ACCEPT THE CHALLENGE

1   Create a list of the ten difficult things you are currently having to endure. Write the list on paper, then burn the list and shout, "These things aren't stopping me!"

2   Write a personal manifesto that describes your why – your inspiration. Describe the people and reasons why you will not give up or give in. Print it out on nice paper and frame it and put it where you can easily see it.

3   Buy yourself a new tool that will help you to "go for it!" on a project you've been putting off.

4   Buy yourself a new set of physical therapy ice packs to put in the freezer for when your muscles hurt. Do this as a prophetic act, a way of saying, "When it hurts, I'm gonna put some ice on it and keep going!"

5   Ask your wife what challenges she's currently enduring. Pray out loud for her to have the strength to keep going!

A MAN WHO GIVES BACK

"A generous person will prosper; whoever refreshes others will be refreshed."

Proverbs 11:25, NIV

JOHN'S STORY: BUILT UP BY MEN WHO GAVE BACK

Keith Jones was a decorated special forces veteran who had become a minister and a counselor. When I was an older teenager, Keith helped me through some difficult times; he was an older man who could speak into my life when the natural father-son tensions made it difficult for me to receive guidance from my dad. When I was in my early twenties, and struggling in my faith, Keith was the man who always made time for me. He would listen to me complain, rant, and confess things that needed confessing. After about twenty minutes, he would just look at me and say, "Are you done?" He'd say something like, "Doesn't that just feel good, to get that all out of your system?" Then he'd laugh, and share profound life-shaping wisdom with me.

When I was suddenly dealing with a girlfriend who was suicidal and navigating an unplanned pregnancy, he coached me on how to proceed with righteousness. When I was trying to make sense of what it meant that I had received a calling to missionary work, he guided me through the choices and decisions I needed to make. When I first began leading in ministry and was struggling with the egos and personalities on the Board, he advised me on exactly what to do, and how to bring godly leadership into a difficult situation. The fact is, I can hardly imagine my life without Keith Jones and the wisdom and mentorship he provided. Keith was a man who had become selfless enough to sow into me and pour into me. His choice to be a man who gave back helped build me into the man I am today.

One such man in the Bible is Barnabas. His story is short, recorded on just a few pages of the book of Acts, but his impact is remembered for eternity. Let's discover more about Barnabas together.

GOD'S MAN: BARNABAS

Barnabas, whose name means "son of encouragement," was a man from the early Christian church who was a shining example of selflessness and compassion. His story, as recorded in the New Testament book of Acts, serves as an inspiration to any of us who endeavor to grow in selflessness and desire to develop the gifts of those around us. Barnabas was born on the island of Cyprus, but he later moved to Jerusalem, where he became a part of the early Christian community. He was known for his generosity and selflessness, selling his land and giving the money to the apostles to help support the needs of the church. One of the most notable things about Barnabas was his ability to encourage and develop others. When

Saul (who later became the apostle Paul) first converted to Christianity, many were skeptical of him because of his past persecution of Christians. But Barnabas saw something in Saul that others did not. He took Saul under his wing and helped him to become an important leader in the early church.

Barnabas' selflessness and encouragement did not stop with Saul. He also played a key role in the development of John Mark, who was Barnabas' cousin. When Paul and Barnabas were on their first missionary journey, Mark decided to leave them and return home. When they were planning their second journey, Paul did not want to bring Mark with them because of his previous abandonment. But Barnabas believed in Mark and wanted to give him a second chance. The two men went their separate ways. Barnabas took Mark with him, while Paul continued his missionary work without them. Barnabas' faith in Mark paid off, as Mark went on to become an important figure in the early church, and he ultimately wrote one of the four gospels. Without Barnabas' encouragement and support, Mark may not have achieved the success he did.

Read the references from the book of Acts to encounter Barnabas' story in scripture.

DIGGING DEEPER: BARNABAS

1   **Read Acts 4:32–37.** What do these verses reveal about the early Christians in general? What do you learn about the kind of man Barnabas was? Even though the description is brief, identify three things about Barnabas that illustrate how he was a man who gave back.

2   **Read Acts 9:22–30.** What kinds of things did early Christian believers have to endure as a result of their commitment to giving back? What seemed to be the highest priority of their generosity? What can you determine about the character of Barnabas from this passage? What role does Barnabas play in the history of God's Kingdom? What does that show you about the possibilities and purpose for your life?

3 **Read Acts 11:19–26.** What actions did the early church believers prioritize, and what was the result? Name at least three more things you learn about Barnabas from this passage. Do these things show up in your life? What's the evidence?

4 **Read Acts 13:13–14 and 15:36–41.** Summarize what happened here. What does that teach you about relationships among Christian men? What can happen even when we do invest in someone (like Barnabas did with Paul)? What was Barnabas' choice in this moment and what did it lead to? (Hint: there are four gospels, and one of them is the Gospel of _____)

YOUR KINGDOM ASSIGNMENT: BECOMING A MAN WHO GIVES BACK

This world is full of takers, brother. Don't be just one more taker. Many men in this world are passive consumers who spend their lives as spectators. Don't be just another one of those kinds of men! Be a man who rises up, takes his place, and gives back. Give back in your community. Give back among your friends. Give back in your church. Give back with your heart, your finances, your time, your care, your attention, your personal investment, your passion, and your love. In order to give back purposefully, you need to have eyes to see – and what you see will present endless give-back opportunities! Let me give you four particular ways you can and should give back as a selfless man of God.

1. SEE A NEED – AND MEET IT!

"If someone has enough money to live well and sees a brother or sister in need but shows no compassion—how can God's love be in that person?" 1 John 3:17 NLT

If you'll open your eyes, you'll notice there are needs all around you. The school your kids attend needs parents who will volunteer in the classroom and for events. Why should you think 'someone else will do it', or 'that's for the moms'? Your city has areas that are dirty, and people who are underserved and under-resourced. Some people will help with needs around Thanksgiving, but what about the rest of the year? Don't just pat yourself on the back because you donated $40 for a turkey once upon a time. Go beyond that! Look for a way you can meet a need on a consistent basis. Isn't this what a king should do? Man of God, open your eyes, ask God to show you the needs, and then meet them!

2. SEE PEOPLE – AND POUR INTO THEM!

"God is not unjust; he will not forget your work and the love you have shown him as you have helped his people and continue to help them." Hebrews 6:10 NIV

You're a man with a lot on your plate. You've got a business or career to build, a ministry to lead, and a family to take care of. Nevertheless, you cannot let your eyes become closed to the value of the people around you. Ask God to give you an open heart to the people around you, and a willingness to help them. We're not just talking about a random occasional handout but a heartfelt willingness to pour into them. This might look like making yourself available to talk with people in need so that you can understand the real dilemma. Maybe they need wisdom or counsel that you could give. Maybe they need you to sponsor the cost of their education for a certain qualification to get a better job. Just know that as you pour into people to help them, your heavenly Father sees and will not forget! Even if the person you pour into doesn't recognize the value (or worse, squanders it and disappoints you), your God sees it all, and calls you to pour into people no matter whether they do well with what you give them or not.

3. SEE A MAN – AND MENTOR HIM!

"And the things you have heard me say in the presence of many witnesses entrust to reliable people who will also be qualified to teach others." 2 Timothy 2:2 NIV

When you consider the scriptures, there are many examples of men who mentored other men. Jethro mentored Moses. Samuel mentored David. Elijah mentored Elisha. Jesus mentored the twelve disciples. Paul mentored Timothy. Brother, you are meant to be a mentor too! One of the best things you could do with your life is mentoring another man as a disciple, as a follower of Jesus. Can you envision it? That's your kingdom assignment! You could provide business mentorship, if that's what's needed.. But here's a practical idea for how you can mentor another man or a group of men: get copies of this book, and give them to a few other guys and say, "Hey, let's meet once a week and go through the discussion questions of this book. I think it will help us both grow and become the kings in God's Kingdom that we are meant to be. Are you in?" Imagine the ripple effect for years to come if you'd do that!

4. SEE THE DARKNESS, AND SHINE INTO IT!

"You are the light of the world—like a city on a hilltop that cannot be hidden. No one lights a lamp and then puts it under a basket. Instead, a lamp is placed on a stand, where it gives light to everyone in the house. In the same way, let your good deeds shine out for all to see, so that everyone will praise your heavenly Father. Matthew 5:14–16 NLT

You don't have to look very hard to see there is a lot of evil and injustice in our world. Terrible things happen on a daily basis. And yet, you're here. You are here, right where you are, with the fire of God burning brightly in you. That fire is light, and Jesus is calling for you to let that light shine into the darkness! Darkness is defeated by the light of Jesus, so shine His light! It has been said that '...all it takes for evil to prevail is for good men to do nothing.' Don't be that man that does nothing. Brother, you do not need to be afraid of the darkness. You need to show up, with Christ in you, right where the shadows are, and shine!

MAN ARISE AS A SELFLESS MAN

In many ways, we are each the product of the people who have been selfless enough to pour into us. Over the course of your life, there have likely been numerous people who have sacrificed their time and given of their wisdom to build you up: teachers in every grade, counselors at camps, coaches, scout leaders, bosses, managers, chiefs, and mentors actively did their part to help you to become the man you are today. And now, we (Skylar and John) want to tell you it's time for you to take your turn in pouring into others.

You already know that God's Word is full of examples of men who poured into other men to see them develop and grow. But you need to remember that these examples exist for you to emulate. Some young men are feeling confused and aimless right now, and God's plan is for you to show up in their lives carrying God's goodness so they can become who God has ordained for them to be. What you'll discover is that in the process, you'll become who God has made you to be, too.

Brother, you are designed to be a pipeline through whom God's goodness and blessings can flow into this world, and into people. Generally speaking, though, this doesn't happen by accident. It happens when you decide that this is the kind of person you want to be. Search your heart and consider how much blessing and favor you've received throughout your life. Decide now that rather than being a cul-de-sac, you're going to be a conduit, and become a man who gives back.

THE REST OF JOHN' STORY:
IT'S THE KEITH JONES TRADITION — AND THE JESUS WAY!

I've had the blessing of being in pastoral ministry for more than 25 years now. One of the greatest joys of my life is seeing young men that I've poured into rise up and discover their calling in ministry. There are numerous guys out there who serve as worship directors, missionaries, and pastors who were part of my ministry team at one time. In each case, there were countless hours of investment — time spent listening, processing, counseling, advising, and praying so that these individuals could grow into what God intended them to be. These men were crucial to the momentum and success of the ministry — and each time, it was difficult to lose them as they went on to what was next for their lives.

The thing is, I know that in my own life, God brought men like Keith Jones into my life to help me grow. I didn't add much value to Keith Jones' life, except for the one time I helped him rip some old carpet out of his house! He poured into me despite the fact that there wasn't much in it for him. As I mentor up & coming ministers now, I do so in keeping with the Keith Jones tradition. I do it because it was what was done for me. I do it because it is the way of the Kingdom of God!

Recently I was at a large gathering of pastors, and Mike, one of my former staff members, was the main speaker for the event. Mike has been leading a church in the Pacific Northwest that has grown to more than 2,000 people. Mike's reputation precedes him because of the fruitfulness and effectiveness of that church. At this event, Mike got up to speak, and he began by saying 'If you gain any value from what I share today, you should know that I learned it from John Hansen, the man of God who mentored me'. We don't always get to see the results of laying down our lives and pouring into others. That day I was blessed to see a glimpse of the goodness that it brought about. But whether I see the impact or not — selflessness is the Jesus way — and I'm determined to keep walking in it by the grace of God!

KINGS DISCUSSION QUESTIONS

1   Share a couple of ways you've 'given back' so far in your life.

Name some of the ways you know you are selfish and how that selfishness gets in the way of you really giving back.

2   **Read Hebrews 13:16, Matthew 5:42–47, and Matthew 25:31–45.** How have you responded to the needs around you in the community or in the church?

Talk about what you WOULD do to help with needs if you could stop making excuses. Name one step you will take this week to start meeting some needs.

3   **Read James 2:14–17, Luke 3:10–11, Matthew 10:8, and Isaiah 58:10.** If you were to apply these verses to your own life, what do the scriptures here call you to?

Talk about someone you know (or have known) who sees and values people and pours into them. What's keeping you from being that kind of man yourself?

4   **Read 2 Timothy 2:2, Proverbs 27:17, Proverbs 13:20, Matthew 28:19–20, Philippians 4:9 and Hebrews 10:24–25.** Name some of the people who have mentored you and have actually discipled you. What was their impact on your life? When are you planning to pay it forward?

Share about two or three men you could imagine discipling, and why they need the guidance, development, or mentoring that you could offer. Talk about how you might even use this book to do it.

5   **Read Isaiah 60:1–5, Psalm 18:28, Matthew 5:14–16 and James 1:17.** What do these verses show you about the need for God's light, the quality of God's light, and the means for God's light to shine?

Where is there some darkness that you've tolerated or shrugged your shoulders about when actually, you're meant to shine God's goodness and love into that place?

ARISE AND ACCEPT THE CHALLENGE

1   Create a 'needs board' on which you write down needs you know about in all the major spheres of your life: family, household, business, church, kids' schools, clubs, city, state, nation, world.

2   Find a place in your city or town to show up and serve selflessly, and do it this week!

3   Make a list of five men you could reach out to with the Rise Up Kings MAN ARISE Bible study. Text, call, or talk to each of them and invite them to join you!

A MAN OF MARITAL MASTERY

*He who finds a wife finds what is good and
receives favor from the LORD.*

Proverbs 18:22

SKYLAR'S STORY

I almost destroyed my marriage before it even started. I fell in love with Jessica the first moment I saw her. Within a week I gave her a bouquet of roses with one rose a different color. My note said, "you're the one in a million and you're the one I want to be with." I had nothing to offer her. I was completely broke. She saw something in me worth taking a chance on. We quickly moved in together. She was very successful even at a young age and she had a trip out of town where she was winning an award for her work. While she was on that trip, I got a text from an ex-girlfriend asking if I wanted to meet up. I knew where that would lead and I accepted. We ended up having sex that night. The feelings of guilt overwhelmed me. I knew if Jessica ever found out it would break her heart. I vowed to never tell her.

Months later, Jessica and I were in marriage counseling. Our counselor told us we needed to come clean with any secrets we were hiding because if we didn't, that secret would take up energy for the rest of our marriage. I knew he was right. I knew what I had to do. I told her. As I expected, she was devastated.

When she was pregnant with our first son, I promised to take two months off to be home with her and the baby. I had worked too many hours for too many years and this would bring some balance. After a couple of weeks, I went back to work. I made a career out of disappointing my wife and frankly, I took her for granted. I didn't love, respect, and cherish her the way I should have.

Considering all the ways I have failed as a husband in the past, I am reminded of an exemplary husband in the Bible: Boaz.

GOD'S MAN: BOAZ

One example of a great husband in the Bible is Boaz. Boaz is portrayed as a wealthy landowner who shows kindness and compassion to Ruth, a widow whom his family was connected with. While not the traditional story of husband and wife, their life together is beautiful and powerful. Boaz models many qualities of a godly husband. Take some time to read through the entire book of Ruth and discover more about this godly example of a husband. You will see that Boaz protects Ruth's rights and ensures her safety, ultimately becoming her husband and the father of her child. Boaz is a model of godly character for men, particularly in regard to his role as a husband. Read all of the book of Ruth in the Bible, then engage with these digging deeper questions.

DIGGING DEEPER: BOAZ

1 **Read Ruth 2:8–9 and Ruth 3:9–13.** What are some qualities of Boaz that make him a good husband?

2 **Read Ruth 2:8–16.** How does Boaz treat Ruth with kindness and respect?

3 **Read Ruth 4:1–10.** In what ways does Boaz show himself to be a worthy husband?

4 How can you apply the lessons you learned from Boaz's life to your own life as a husband?

5 Write down one thing that stood out to you or that came to your mind as you read this chapter, as it pertains to you becoming a man who is learning to husband well.

YOUR KINGDOM ASSIGNMENT: RISING UP AS A MAN WHO "HUSBANDS" WELL!

Take some time to familiarize yourself with these six priorities of husbanding well. Allow these six elements to become definitive for you as you consider what it means to husband well! Being a great husband is not just a matter of circumstance or luck, but rather a deliberate choice. As Christian men, we are called to love and serve our wives in a way that reflects the love of Christ. These six priorities will help you do that!

SIX PRIORITIES FOR HUSBANDS

1. LOVE UNCONDITIONALLY

"Husbands, love your wives, just as Christ loved the church and gave himself up for her" Ephesians 5:25 NIV

The first and most important thing you must do as a Christian husband is to love your wife unconditionally, just as Christ loves us. This means loving her when she is at her best and at her worst, and always putting her needs before your own.

2. COMMUNICATE EFFECTIVELY

"Let your conversation be always full of grace, seasoned with salt, so that you may know how to answer everyone." Colossians 4:6 NIV

Communication is key to any successful relationship, and a Christian husband must be an effective communicator. This means actively listening to your wife, expressing your feelings in a healthy way, and working together to resolve conflicts.

3. LEAD SPIRITUALLY

"For the husband is the head of the wife as Christ is the head of the church, his body, of which he is the Savior. Now as the church submits to Christ, so also wives should submit to their husbands in everything." Ephesians 5:23–24 NIV

As a Christian husband, you must lead your wife and family in spiritual growth and development. This means setting a good example through personal worship and devotion to Jesus, and encouraging your wife and children to grow in their relationship with God.

4. LIVE SACRIFICIALLY

"Do nothing out of selfish ambition or vain conceit. Rather, in humility value others above yourselves, not looking to your own interests but each of you to the interests of the others." Philippians 2:3–4 NIV

A great husband must be willing to sacrifice his own interests and desires for the sake of his wife and family. This means putting your wife first, being selfless, and always acting in the best interests of your bride. This means you will be setting aside some of your own wants, desires, and preferences — and doing that without any sorry-faced sulking!

5. RELATE INTENTIONALLY

"Husbands, in the same way be considerate as you live with your wives, and treat them with respect as the weaker partner and as heirs with you of the gracious gift of life, so that nothing will hinder your prayers." 1 Peter 3:7 NIV

Brother, you must be intentional in your actions and decisions, always striving to make the most of your time and resources. This means planning ahead, setting goals, and working hard to achieve them, all while prioritizing your relationship with your wife and family. Relating intentionally includes the priority of establishing a sense of safety and reliability for your wife.

6. ENGAGE ROMANTICALLY

"My beloved is mine and I am his; he browses among the lilies." Song of Solomon 2:16

An amazing husband will do his part to actively cultivate romance in the marriage. He will engage in ways that show deep, intimate connection. He will initiate physical intimacy in ways that are passionate and yet tender.

There are many more things that a Christian husband can do to be an awesome husband, but these six are a great starting point. Whether you are just starting out in your journey as a husband, or you have been married for many years, these principles can help guide you towards a stronger, more loving relationship with your wife.

MAN ARISE AS A MAN OF MARITAL MASTERY

When you were a child, you probably went through a phase where 'girls were gross.' Even that phrase takes you somewhere in your mind, doesn't it? Eventually, you discovered that not only were girls not gross, they were pretty awesome. You probably arrived at that insight once hormones kicked in, so yeah, you had some help. Nevertheless, you came to the right conclusion! After some years passed, you determined that you'd want to be married one day, to embrace a woman as your wife. You may have had a picture in the back of your mind of the kind of woman you'd want to marry. You may have even written down a list of the kinds of qualities and attributes you hoped your one-day wife might have.

And then it happened. You met her. You swept her off her feet, and she knocked you off of yours, right into the life of love! You had a time of wonderful courtship and dating. You wooed her with gifts. Your heart was warm towards her all the time — and physically — well, warm doesn't even come close to describing what was going on there. You might have been a Christian at the time and if you were, you prayed, and God confirmed to you that she was the one. Or you simply thanked God that you'd determined she was!

You waited until just the right moment. You took that ring you bought with money you'd worked hard to save, and you proposed. She said yes. Pictures were taken, smiles and celebrations followed that moment and are still a part of your biography together with her. A date was set and maybe you got in a couple of premarital counseling sessions. She planned a wedding and somebody probably advised you to let her take charge of that for the most part. And if you listened to that advice you avoided some serious pitfalls! If you never got that advice, you discovered pretty quickly that a wife-to-be is a force not to be reckoned with regarding the wedding day!

You survived the wedding planning and you made it to the big day. Perhaps you did something uber-romantic in the days leading up to the wedding — a special gift, a private beautiful moment... or maybe you just barely made it to the ceremony. Maybe you skipped all of the above and eloped or came together in some even less traditional way. But it happened. The knot was tied, the vows were spoken, and the two became one. The two became one.

From God's perspective, that is what happened the moment those vows were exchanged in His presence. From that moment on you have been one flesh with your wife. This union is unique; it is a partnership unlike any other. There is an intended degree of intimacy that is unrivaled in any other relationship on earth. You have enjoyed wonderful highs with this woman you've married and you may have also endured some times of awful tension and desperation, sometimes with her, and sometimes because of her. And yet, here you are, a man who understands that this oneness is an absolute gift from God!

You are called to husband well. Yes, we're using 'husband' as a verb. Of course it doesn't show up in the dictionary that way, but it should. You accepted a noble calling when you vowed to be her husband. And you need to know that she has a Father in Heaven who has His eye on you. He's full of grace but he does expect you to do right by His beloved daughter!

THE REST OF THE STORY

When I told Jessica about cheating on her, it broke her heart. She was emotionally devastated. She rightly reasoned that if I would do this while we were dating, what would stop me from doing it after we were married? She wondered if I really loved her and was committed to her. It took her a long time to come to terms with it. Ultimately, she decided to forgive me and accept me as her husband. What a grace she gave me!

I wish that was the last time I disappointed her. It was the last time I disappointed her with cheating but I later disappointed her by using porn, struggling with alcohol, and, as I shared before, not taking the time I promised to be home with our first baby.

By God's grace, and Jessica's grace, I show up better today. I am growing and I live up to my word most of the time! Even today, I drop the ball when I don't listen intently to her when she is sharing her feelings. By their grace, I walk in freedom from pornography, seek to live by the principles in this chapter, and I am still improving in work/life priorities. My marriage has been restored and I now help thousands of couples create marriages that truly glorify God. It is time that we become lights in this dark world.

KINGS DISCUSSION QUESTIONS

1   From the list of 'six priorities for a husband' written above, which one do you feel you excel the most at, and how have you learned to do that well?

   Which of the 'six priorities' would your wife say she feels you do well?

2   From the list of 'six priorities for a husband' written above, which one do you feel you most need to work on?

   Why is this particular area of priority as a husband something you struggle with?

3   **Read Ephesians 5:21, Ephesians 5:25, and Ephesians 5:33.** How do these verses apply to a husband's role in loving his wife? What does this type of love look like in action?

   What step are you going to take this week to put that into practice?

4   **Read Colossians 3:8–10, Colossians 4:6, James 1:19–20, and Ephesians 4:29.** How can these passages be used as a guide for effective communication in a marriage? What steps can you take to be a better listener and communicator as a husband?

Share about where you've failed in communication as a husband.

4   **Read 1 Peter 3:7.** What can you learn from this about leading your family spiritually? What can you do to inspire and encourage your wife spiritually and spur spiritual growth in your marriage?

Share about why it may sometimes be a struggle for you to do this.

5   **Read Philippians 2:1–4.** What do these words show you about sacrifice in a marriage? How can you put this principle into action in your daily life as a husband?

What gets in the way of you living sacrificially as a husband?

6   **Read Ephesians 5:15–16.** What would it look like for you to apply this scripture to your role as a husband when it comes to being intentional in your actions and decisions? What steps can you take to prioritize your relationship with your wife and family?

   🛡 *Be real and share about the ways you tend to be careless about your marriage. Where do you feel conviction about how you've been thoughtless about your marriage or treated your wife as an afterthought?*

7   **Read Song of Solomon 2:16 and consider how you can engage more romantically with your wife.** What are some of the things SHE would probably like you to do to be more romantic with her?

   🛡 *What are you choosing INSTEAD of romance for and with your wife?*

ARISE AND ACCEPT THE CHALLENGE:

1   Choose one item on the list of priorities of a godly husband and write an action step to commit to that priority with greater love and effectiveness.

2   Buy a gift for your wife this week, and give it to her with a note that describes how she is beautiful and why you love her.

3   Initiate a time of intimacy that begins with affection, warmth, and romance and continues to mutual fulfillment!

FURTHER STUDY:
Ephesians 5:21–33; Matthew 19:6; Malachi 2:15; Ecclesiastes 9:9; Genesis 2:24; 1 Corinthians 7:1–5; Proverbs 5:18–19; 1 Peter 3:7

A MAN OF PATERNAL STRENGTH

"And I will be your Father, and you will be my sons and daughters, says the Lord Almighty."

2 Corinthians 6:18

JOHN'S STORY: CULTIVATING PATERNAL STRENGTH

There is one thing you and I have in common, no matter what other differences there are between us: we have fathers. Yours may have been fantastic, hurtful, distant, kind, cruel, or absent but you were brought into this world because there was a man who caused your life to begin. That man and everything about him has left a permanent mark on you, for better or for worse. And now you stand as a man who may be a father or as a man who is preparing to be one. You might have even graduated to grandfather status. Whether your status as a father is current or something you aspire to, the task of fatherhood is one of the greatest responsibilities you could ever assume.

My experience with my dad was somewhat unique. My father contracted the Polio virus when he was fourteen years old, and it left him paralyzed from the waist down for the rest of his life. In case you're wondering, no, his 'manhood' was not paralyzed, and he gave my mother three naturally-born offspring! But he did walk upright only with the assistance of canes and metal leg braces and crutches; otherwise, he was in a wheelchair. His paralysis robbed him just as he was becoming a man himself. It robbed him of his dignity, his mobility, his social standing, and his ability in many ways. This robbery left my dad angry and he carried that anger into his adulthood, and into his fatherhood.

When I was a kid, I often saw my dad burst out in rage in all kinds of different circumstances. I saw the veins in his neck pop out, I heard the volume and intensity of his voice escalate, and I understood exactly what he meant when he would shout every word in the book (and I'm not talking about the Bible!) It caused fear to rise up in my young soul. His explosiveness was fueled by a deep sense of injustice; his paralysis and the loss of his mobility was awful. The way many in his family ostracized him was wrong. The pity with which many people looked at him was humiliating and the infuriation of it all seemed to lurk just beneath the surface. Countless times my dad, unable to run after me, would hurl objects at me – keys, tools, a log, a book. If he was close enough, I would catch the back side of his hand. I don't blame him; I was probably screwing around and deserved to be corrected. But his unbridled anger went far beyond what would have been healthy parenting. And the impact of my father's own wounded spirit left me wounded in ways that I wouldn't come to deal with until I was about to have kids of my own.

The problem is that when men don't work through the wrongs done to them by their fathers they tend to pass along the pain and damage to their kids. When this happens, the image of God that a father is meant to reflect to his kids gets distorted. Sons and daughters can end up with a warped view of God because of what they've experienced with their earthly father. I want you to find a way to heal from what hurt you so you can be the kind of man — the kind of father — the kind of king God intends for you to be!

GOD'S MAN: ABRAHAM

One example of a great father in the Bible is Abraham. He is referred to as 'the father of faith', and he is widely regarded as a great father for a multitude of reasons. First and foremost, he was a man of unwavering faith who trusted in God's promises and obeyed His commands even when they were difficult. This faith led him to leave his homeland and travel to an unknown land with his family, demonstrating his willingness to follow God's call no matter the cost. Abraham's devotion to God set an example for his children and future generations to follow, inspiring them to also have faith in God and His plans for their lives. Abraham's industrious approach to life led to the creation of generational wealth and provided a foundation of strength for his family line. Abraham was the grandfather of the man who gave the world the twelve tribes of Israel.

DIGGING DEEPER: ABRAHAM

1 **Read Genesis 12:1–4 and Romans 4:3.** How did Abraham respond when God called him to leave his home and follow Him? How can we respond to God's call and be great fathers?

2 **Read Genesis 18:18–19.** What steps can you take to emulate Abraham with regard to giving a foundation of faith to your kids?

3   **Read Genesis 21:8–14.** How did Abraham prioritize doing what was right over his own feelings? How can we follow Abraham's example in how we make difficult decisions for the good of our families? Is there a difficult decision you sense God prompting you to make for the sake of your family and your kids?

4   **Read Genesis 24:1–9.** Abraham instructed his servant to find a wife for Isaac. How did Abraham prioritize finding a godly spouse for his son, and how can we help our children find godly spouses?

YOUR KINGDOM ASSIGNMENT: BECOME A GODLY FATHER!

Being a great father is not just about having the title 'Dad'; it's a calling. As a Christian man, you are called to lead your family with grace, love, and wisdom, reflecting the image of our Heavenly Father. Embrace your role as a king in your home and lead your family with the same love and compassion that Jesus Christ has shown you! I want to give you six key factors you need to put in place to be an amazing father. The acrostic is TAGGED and I am praying that your kids will be tagged for good by your fathering!

TIME

Children need our time and attention, and it is our responsibility as fathers to give them both. We must be present in our children's lives, carving out time to engage with them in meaningful ways. This means putting down our phones and other distractions, and actively listening to our children when they speak to us. When we spend time with our children, we build a foundation of trust and respect, which is crucial to our relationship with them.

"And he will turn the hearts of the fathers to the children, and the hearts of the children to their fathers" Malachi 4:6 NKJV

AFFECTION

Children need to know that they are loved unconditionally, and it is our role as fathers to show them that love through our words and actions. This means expressing affection, offering words of encouragement and affirmation, and giving plenty of hugs and physical affection. When we show affection to our children, we create a sense of belonging and acceptance that is essential to their emotional and spiritual well-being.

"Jesus said, "Let the little children come to me, and do not hinder them, for the kingdom of heaven belongs to such as these." When he had placed his hands on them, he went on from there." Matthew 19:14–15 NIV

GUIDANCE

Children need guidance and direction as they navigate the challenges of life, and it is our role as fathers to provide wise counsel and support. This means being available to listen, offering practical advice, and pointing our children to the wisdom of God's Word. When we provide guidance to our children, we help them to develop a sense of purpose and direction that is grounded in truth and wisdom.

"Fathers, do not provoke your children to anger, but bring them up in the discipline and instruction of the Lord." Ephesians 6:4 NIV

GRACE

Children need to experience grace and forgiveness, especially when they make mistakes or fall short of our expectations. As fathers, we have the opportunity to model the grace and forgiveness of Christ to our children, offering them the same unconditional love and acceptance that we have received from our Heavenly Father. This means being quick to forgive, showing compassion and understanding, and extending mercy even when it is not deserved. When we offer grace to our children, we create an environment of trust and safety that is essential for their growth and development. Grace is more than just forgiveness; it's giving your children good things that they didn't earn. When we buy gifts for our children and play with them and encourage them and bless them – not as a reward for good behavior, but because we love them – we are teaching them about the love of God that flows from who He is, not from how we can please Him.

"Fathers, do not embitter your children, or they will become discouraged." Colossians 3:21 NIV

EMPATHY

Children need to know that we understand their feelings and emotions, and that we care about what they are going through. This means being emotionally available, listening attentively, and showing compassion and understanding. When we demonstrate empathy to our children, we build a deeper level of trust and connection that is vital to our relationship with them.

"As a father has compassion on his children, so the Lord has compassion on those who fear him." Psalm 103:13 NIV

DISCIPLINE

Children need boundaries and structure in their lives, and it is our responsibility as fathers to provide these things in a loving and consistent manner. This means setting clear expectations and consequences, and following through with them when necessary. Discipline should always be done in a way that is respectful and compassionate, never harsh or demeaning. Discipline should lead to genuine repentance, not just realizing that bad choices lead to bad consequences. When we discipline our children well, we help them to develop self-control and responsibility, which are essential life skills.

"Whoever spares the rod hates their children, but the one who loves their children is careful to discipline them." Proverbs 13:24 NIV

MAN ARISE AS A MAN OF PATERNAL STRENGTH

As men of God, we are called to reflect His image in all aspects of our lives, including being a father. Being a great father is not just about providing for your family, but also about being a spiritual leader and a guiding light in your children's lives. As a father, you hold a position of great responsibility and honor, and you are called to lead your family with grace, strength, and wisdom.

The Bible reminds us of our worth as children of God and our royal status in passages like 1 Peter 2:9, where it says, "But you are a chosen people, a royal priesthood, a holy nation, God's special possession, that you may declare the praises of him who called you out of darkness into his wonderful light." In the same way that a king leads his kingdom, you are called to lead your family with love, compassion, and a servant's heart.

It's important to remember that as a father, you are not only responsible for your children's physical needs, but also their spiritual growth. You are to be a spiritual mentor, teaching them about God's love and giving them spiritual guidance. Deuteronomy 6:4–9 reminds us, "Hear, O Israel: The Lord our God, the Lord is one. Love the Lord your God with all your heart and with all your soul and with all your strength. These commandments that I give you today are to be upon your hearts. Impress them on your children. Talk about them when you sit at home and when you walk along the road, when you lie down and when you get up." This is a picture of the way you are called to prioritize providing godly spiritual influence for your kids.

Just as a coach trains an athlete, you are called to train your children in the ways of the Lord. In Colossians 3:21, it says, "Fathers, do not embitter your children, or they will become discouraged." This means that you must approach parenting with patience and understanding, leading your children with a gentle hand. It's also important to remember that being a great father requires effort and sacrifice. Just as a farmer invests time and energy into his crops, you must invest time and energy into your kids. Finally, like a shepherd cares for his flock, you are called to care for your kids. Lead them with wisdom and guidance, always striving to be an example of Christ's love.

THE REST OF JOHN'S STORY: A FATHER CAN ARISE IN GRACE

Around the time when I trusted Jesus Christ for salvation when I was 14 years old, my Dad came to know Christ as his Savior as well. A man in the neighborhood named Yoshio had a woodshop in his garage fully stocked with excellent finish carpentry tools. My dad would sometimes take a slow walk around the block with his leg braces and canes. That woodshop and Yoshio's craftsmanship caught my dad's attention on one of those walks. He invited my dad in to see the shop, and they worked on some woodworking projects together. Yoshio became a friend to my father. Yoshio was a Christian and over time, he shared about Jesus with my Dad.

My Dad had been trained as a lawyer and he was a fierce debater. His veins would flare with rage as he rebutted Yoshio's claims about Christ, the Bible, and eternal truth. But Yoshio was persistent. His notable skill in apologetics earned my dad's respect. His excellence as a woodworker and his hospitality engaged my father's heart. Through this friendship and my mother's encouragement for them to try a new church, my dad gave his life to Christ, and his transformation began.

Over the following years, I saw the rage that used to be so common in my father give way to gentleness and self control. He became more gracious, more patient, and more tender. It didn't happen overnight but it happened, and I saw it. Witnessing that transformation in my father changed me! When I was 18 years old I left home, basically for good. I had a year of travel and adventure planned and I didn't permanently live at home again. But the day I left will always stand out in my memory. My dad was going to bring me to the train station to begin my journey. The beige station wagon was in the driveway and my backpack was stowed in the back.

Before getting in the car, my dad leaned against the car to support himself, and then flung one arm wide open gesturing for a hug. This wasn't really very common for my Dad, a man who'd been raised in the farmlands of Iowa by stoic midwesterners of the WW2 generation. He threw his arm around me, said 'I love you, John!' He held me, and wept aloud. This moment lasted something like five minutes. On one level, it marked the finality of my season of living at home. At another level, though, it represented the dramatic change that had taken place in my own father because of the power of Christ. He had become a father through whom grace and tenderness could flow in a way that just wasn't possible without Jesus.

I'll always be grateful for the difference God's grace made in my own father's life. It's proof that God's transforming power is real, and that His grace is powerful! It's evidence that a father can grow and change, and shift the unhealthy cycles that one generation tends to pass to the next. I saw my own dad arise in grace, and it gave me a testimony of what my God can do!

◊ KINGS DISCUSSION QUESTIONS

1   Which of the six TAGGED elements are you doing well? Share an example.

   ◊ *Why do you think you excel at this one particular factor of great fatherhood?*

2   Which of the TAGGED fatherhood factors was something you did not receive from your father, or experienced in a negative way from your father?

   ◊ *Which of the TAGGED fatherhood factors are you missing the mark on right now in your own fathering? What are you going to do about it?*

3   **Read Deuteronomy 6:4–9 and Malachi 4:6.** What do these verses reveal about a father's efforts to guide his children towards a life of faith?

   ◊ *How much time are you personally spending in building up your kids' faith, and what are some examples of how you do that?*

4   **Read Colossians 3:21 and Matthew 19:14–15.** What does the scripture here teach us about the importance of a gentle approach to parenting? What is the role and purpose of healthy affection in fathering?

> *Do you think your children are getting enough attention and affection from you? What's in the way — and what are you going to do about it?*

5   **Read Hebrews 12:7–11, Proverbs 23:13–14, and Proverbs 3:11–12.** What makes disciplining your children difficult? What would happen if you took 'discipline' too far with your kids? What would happen if you didn't discipline your kids?

> *How have you messed up when disciplining your kids?*

6   **Read Ephesians 6:4 and Proverbs 22:6.** How did your own father provide guidance to you?

> *How have you struggled — or succeeded — in providing guidance for your kids. What is your plan for giving more good guidance moving forward?*

ARISE AND ACCEPT THE CHALLENGE

1   Schedule a daddy-daughter or father-son hang time for the next week. Tell your wife and child about it and make a plan for it.

2   Do 10/10 faith building challenge with your child or kids: each day, for ten days straight, spend ten minutes with your child engaging in spiritual development. Read a bible verse together, pray together, or even worship together! Look for ways in everyday activities to bring your children's attention to God, God's love and provision for us, and God's desire that we live righteous lives that bless others.

3   Have a sit-down with your wife to discuss discipline and ask her: "Are we on the same page regarding how we discipline our kids? Do you feel you'd like to see me make any adjustments in my approach to discipline with them?'

A MAN WHO LEADS WELL

"If God has given you leadership ability, take the responsibility seriously."

Romans 12:8, NLT

JOHN'S STORY: EXPERIENCING THE IMPACT OF LEADERSHIP

Can you remember the first time in your life you experienced leadership? I have foggy recollections of moments in a classroom, playing something like 'Simon Says' and experiencing something like leadership. I have faint memories of a summer camp counselor arranging us kids into teams to play 'red rover.' You could say that was leadership. I joined Cub Scouts and a den mother got all us boys in the pack to help with a community clean-up day. Leadership. These are some of my earliest memories of leadership and you probably have plenty of your own memories like that.

At some point, leadership was about more than playing games or doing a project. You and I have experiences of being led well or led poorly into moments of much greater importance: a coach who led a team all the way to the championships; a boss who led the company that gave you your first taste of success; a captain, chief or commander who ensured your division found a path to victory. From your own experience you can understand how much good leadership matters.

The Bible is absolutely filled with examples of excellent and terrible leadership. The word 'leadership' is not used often but demonstrations of leadership abound. In the Bible, the term 'shepherding' is often used as a metaphor for leadership. For example, Psalm 23 says, "The Lord is my Shepherd...", and the prophets refer to the judges and kings as 'the shepherds of Israel'. The prophets themselves were leaders among God's people, effecting change and catalyzing future results through their stature, boldness, godliness, and strong communication.

In the scriptures there are many amazing leaders. Peter was deputized by Jesus to lead the Church after the Resurrection. Paul became the apostolic leader who brought the gospel from the Middle East to Europe, starting and leading a movement of hundreds of churches along the way. David was a king whose leadership united the twelve tribes. Abraham led his family and workers to enter into the promised land, and so did Joshua, again, years later. But one of the greatest examples of leadership is found in Moses. Let's take some time to get to know God's man, Moses.

GOD'S MAN: MOSES

Moses is one of the most important figures in the Hebrew Bible and is recognized as a prophet, leader, and lawgiver to the Israelites. He was born in Egypt during a time when the Israelites were being oppressed and enslaved by the Pharaoh. According to the biblical account, Moses was chosen by God to lead the Israelites out of slavery and into the Promised Land. He is believed to have lived during the 13th century BC, which was a time of political instability in Egypt and the Near East.

Moses' achievements as a leader are numerous and include his role in the Ten Plagues of Egypt, the Exodus, the parting of the Red Sea, the reception of the Ten Commandments on Mount Sinai, and the establishment of the Israelites as a nation. He is also known for his ability to communicate with God and his role in leading the Israelites through the wilderness for forty years. His leadership was not without challenges, however, as he had to deal with his own self-doubt and guilt feelings, not to mention rebellions, complaints, and doubts from his people. Moses' story is recorded in the books of Exodus, Leviticus, Numbers, and Deuteronomy in the Hebrew Bible. You may not have the time to read all of those books of the Bible but to get a good sense of Moses' life, read in Exodus 3 about 'the burning bush.' Read in Exodus 14 about the parting of the Red Sea. Read in Exodus 18 about the leadership wisdom from Jethro. Read in Exodus 20 about the Ten Commandments. Reference these sections as you dig deeper.

DIGGING DEEPER: MOSES

1   **Read Exodus 3.** How does God's call to Moses demonstrate the challenges and realities of accepting a call to leadership? How does God's call to Moses highlight qualities of an effective leader? What are some of those qualities you see in Moses? What can you learn from Moses' response to God's call?

2   **Read Exodus 14.** How did Moses demonstrate trust in God's plan despite the seemingly impossible situation the Israelites were facing? How did the people react to Moses' leadership and what does that indicate about the nature of leading people? What did Moses do in this moment? Can you identify his leadership actions?

3   **Read Exodus 18.** What did Moses learn about team building, delegation, and the importance of wise counsel? How can you apply this lesson to your own leadership style?

4   **Read Exodus 20.** How did Moses effectively communicate the Ten Commandments to the Israelites? What can you learn from his approach to teaching and leading the people? What challenges did he encounter with his communications initiatives? What does this teach you about leadership, vision, and communication?

YOUR KINGDOM ASSIGNMENT: BECOME A GODLY LEADER!

The purpose of leadership is to motivate people to work together to solve a problem and create positive outcomes and success. Whether in your business, an organization where you serve, your church, or in a civic role, leadership is needed. It's time for you to rise up, king! Being a king is about walking with impact in this world, and part of how you will do that for the glory of God is by stepping up your leadership whenever you have the opportunity! The following are the five essential actions of leadership. If you ever wondered what the formula is for leadership, this is it. Study them, engage in understanding the biblical foundations for each, and look for the opportunities to put them into practice!

1 – CONFIDENTLY CREATE COMPELLING VISION

"Where there is no vision, the people perish" Proverbs 29:18 KJV

As a leader, it's your job to create a vision that solves a problem. If you see a problem and have a solution, you are in the realm of vision. Think through your idea. Consider how your solution is the answer to the problem or the pain point in the organization or in the community. At the core, that's what vision does; it solves a problem and presents a preferred future that is possible when that solution is implemented. Leadership starts with seeing the possible solution to a problem, and talking about that preferred future in a way that people can imagine the good that is possible. But brother, your personal confidence is part of how people will feel compelled by the vision, so stir up your own heart with confidence in who God has called you to be and in the vision you have!

2 – DECISIVELY ESTABLISH STRATEGY AND ORCHESTRATION

"Strategic planning is the key to warfare; to win, you need a lot of good counsel." Proverbs 24:6 MSG

You came up with a solution for a problem. That was your vision. Your next step is to establish a strategy for how the solution can be implemented. You must think through the who, what, when, where and how of your vision — at least at a top-level. Who will be doing what? Where are they doing it? How does it need to be done? And when does each element need to be done? You have a strategy and then you need to orchestrate that strategy. The essence of orchestration is to lay out a draft timeline of who is doing what, and by when. As questions arise, you need to be decisive; if you are wishy-washy, the plan and outcome will be too. Pray, trust your intuition, and be decisive. Don't let yourself get paralyzed over the scope of possibilities. Choose. Decide. Someone has to, and it should be you at this stage, because you are the leader who is establishing the strategy.

3 – COMMUNICATE WITH CLARITY AND MOTIVATION

"Then the Lord answered me and said: "Write the vision, and make it plain on tablets, that he may run who reads it. For the vision is yet for an appointed time; But at the end it will speak, and it will not lie. Though it tarries, wait for it; Because it will surely come, It will not tarry." Habakkuk 2:2–3 NKJV

This verse is ultimately about God's vision for His people to live by faith. But the principle is eternal — and effective. The vision must be communicated with clarity! Figure out how to speak about your vision as clearly as you can. Write it down, then edit it and refine it. Define the problem. Explain the solution. State why the solution matters, and why the end result is going to be worth the effort. Help people feel some kind of emotion about this idea, this vision. They need to feel agitated or upset and discontent with the current reality, and they need to feel excited about the proposed plan. You need to communicate that vision with clarity. People will be motivated and engaged by their emotional connection to the vision. They will be clear on the "Why" behind the plan!

4 – INSPIRE COMMITMENT AND TEAMWORK BASED ON TRUST

"Two people are better off than one, for they can help each other succeed. If one person falls, the other can reach out and help. But someone who falls alone is in real trouble. Likewise, two people lying close together can keep each other warm. But how can one be warm alone? A person standing alone can be attacked and defeated, but two can stand back-to-back and conquer. Three are even better, for a triple-braided cord is not easily broken." Ecclesiastes 4:9–12 NLT

If you say you're a leader, but you look and there's no one following behind you, you're just a man out taking a walk. As a leader, you must call together the people who will run with your vision and make it happen. If you try to accomplish your vision all by yourself, you're not following the way of Jesus, and you're not going to have much impact. You must invite people to be part of your team. You have to inspire them with the vision, and build relationships of trust with people. Trust is the foundation of teamwork and as the leader, it is your job to cultivate it. There is no shortcut; relationships take time, attention, respect, and connection. You've probably heard the phrase: 'teamwork makes the dream work!' It may sound superficial but it's the truth. Once you gather a team, and cultivate relationships and trust, there needs to be a clear moment when you ask for people to make a commitment to the vision. That can be as simple as a verbal, "So are you in?" or as extensive as a signed document. As the leader, this is what you do; you inspire commitment and teamwork based on trust!

5 – CATALYZE ACTION AND MOMENTUM THROUGH EMPOWERMENT

"This is not good!" Moses' father-in-law exclaimed. "You're going to wear yourself out—and the people, too. This job is too heavy a burden for you to handle all by yourself... But select from all the people some capable, honest men who fear God and hate bribes. Appoint them as leaders over groups of one thousand, one hundred, fifty, and ten."
Exodus 17:18–19; 21 NLT

Think about Jesus Christ for a moment. Of course you are grateful for the Cross and the empty tomb, yes! Now consider this. If Jesus hadn't catalyzed action and momentum through empowerment, there would be no Church as we know it. Jesus modeled empowerment of others. He made an impact on the world by discipling twelve key men and then releasing them to carry His Message. God used Moses' father-in-law to correct his poor leadership and to provide the wisdom for the empowerment of others. As a leader, you must make it a priority to build relationships and then develop people who know that they have a role to play with actions they must take — and that they have the authority to do it. Whenever you are attempting to move something forward, remember this phrase: 'lead through.' Who does God want you to develop and empower to move the vision forward?

MAN ARISE AS A MAN WHO LEADS WELL

One of the preeminent demonstrations of leadership in the Bible is in the kings of Israel. The books of 1 and 2 Kings detail roughly 42 kings of Israel and, notably, 34 of them are awful. The bad kings gave bad leadership to God's people. This caused division, military losses, spiritual demise, and death! Only eight of the Kings were regarded as good kings. It seems unfathomable that among God's chosen people, the vast majority of the leaders were so ineffective and even harmful, but that is the case.

When I read through that part of the Bible, there is something inside of me that wants to say, "Come on, men! Do something about this evil ruler! Where are the godly leaders and rulers? Where are the good kings? When are the good kings going to step up? Come on, rise up, kings!" That was generally the cry of the prophets of the Old Testament and a prophetic voice is being stirred up now with that same cry. That's the reason you're reading this book.

At the core, leadership is about influence, as John Maxwell has said. But most of us know — intuitively, or from experience – that there is more to it than that. Leadership is harnessing your own personal intelligence, energy, presence, and social currency with people to motivate them to work together to accomplish something, often something difficult or something that includes change. Leadership takes intentionality, skill, courage, and endurance. Leadership also requires thick skin, grit, and a lot of stamina.

Rise Up Kings is a movement! It is about you catching a sense of God's call on your life to rise up in your royal identity in Christ and take your place at the table of leadership in this world. Can you hear it? It's as though even now, the Spirit of God is saying to men, "Rise up, kings! This world needs you to rise up with godly leadership! The legacy of your family depends on it. The quality of your community depends on it. The very durability of your society depends on it. So RISE UP KINGS! Rise up and learn to lead in godly, effective ways!"

THE REST OF JOHN'S STORY

I was just 29 years old when I first came to Murrieta. I had been serving as the worship and youth pastor of a wonderful church in Santa Barbara where I was also working as the campus worship pastor for Westmont College. I had been a co-leader of a college fellowship group at Rutgers University called InterVarsity Christian fellowship. I had been a sales manager in a small marketing company. All of these roles afforded me some degree of leadership training and experience, but nothing could have quite prepared me for the leadership challenge I was about to embrace.

I had never been a lead pastor before, but my wife and I moved to this new community to embrace the challenge of relaunching a small, struggling church. I met with the Board President at a diner for the initial interview. He told me about the wonderful history of the church. The founding pastor, Marty Edwards, was something of a legend in the town. The church He started had grown significantly in his tenure, and the congregation carried a sense of passion for Jesus that reflected his own earnest desire for God's Kingdom. The founder's leadership legacy was truly legendary. I would be walking into the deep valley of this man's shadow.

Jim also told me about how the church had come to the place where it was gravely struggling. There had been a terrible church split that scarred the congregation. Then the beloved founder left and started a new parachurch ministry. The next pastor who came in only lasted a year and a half before he lost heart, because the vibrant church had lost so much momentum. Several other treasured team members were let go due to financial constraints. The few church members who remained were disheartened and hurt. There were barely more than 50 people gathering on Sunday mornings.

At this point there was a vacuum of clear leadership; the Board was running the church, and praying for a miracle. Jim described to me how the finances were in the red: the treasurer was at the point of needing to decide which bills wouldn't get paid each month. The rented storefront suite where the church met was becoming especially difficult to afford. Jim shared that he felt the Board wouldn't mind taking a chance on me, even though I'd never been a lead pastor before, because, in his words, they were "...thinking about closing the doors anyway. What's the worst you could do?"

That week, before the leadership had even formally offered me the call to come be the new pastor, something surprising happened. I went to the 10 acre property the church owned. The Board was considering parceling it off to sell, in order to fund the ministry. The property had two dilapidated houses, a shed or two, and a mobile trailer that was falling apart. The place was an eyesore; it was clear vagrants and vandals were using the property as a place to hide out and do drugs. Trash and drug paraphernalia were strewn all around the houses. Windows were crashed out, ceilings were caving in, and the doors were literally swinging in the wind. It seemed to me that the state of the property was as dismal as the state of the congregation who owned it.

I walked to the middle of the property, knelt down, and put my hands onto the ground. My fingers sunk into the loamy soil in an area that had formerly been a horse pen. I began to pray, asking God if it was his will for me to be called as the new pastor for this small church that was wondering if it would even survive. Then and there, God spoke to me and gave me an open vision: I saw a fluid moving picture of this mighty congregation, a huge crowd of people worshiping Jesus there. It was a community full of joy, full of hope, and full of the Spirit. The gathering was in a beautiful large new place. I heard the Lord say to me, "Be strong and do the work! Get ready to be strong and do the work; this is what I spoke to you about when I called you away from Santa Barbara! Be strong and do the work! I have a new identity for this congregation, a new place, a new name, new life, New Impact! Be strong and do the work!"

A leadership mantle was transferred to me at that moment.

In the process that followed, there were interviews and negotiations. Ultimately an offer to come to work for this small church as its new lead pastor. The position was offered to me and the leadership mantle was placed upon me. I willingly stepped into it. There was a profound sense of calling and vision for that calling. It fired me up for the initial challenge, and it has fueled me for the long haul. I knew there was a calling I had stepped into, not just a new position or opportunity.

Men of God come into leadership roles in a variety of ways. There may be a promotion to a new position, a job offer with greater levels of responsibility, or an entrepreneurial endeavor that pays off. The scope of authority and responsibility becomes almost endless. Sometimes it is in a volunteer environment, the needs match your abilities, and you are asked to step into a role which calls for you to lead. As a Man of God, whenever you step into a leadership opportunity, remember who you are. You are a man of God, and men of God lead from a place of calling, not just because there is an opportunity. Carrying out your leadership in business, church, or other organizations from a place of calling gives you profound confidence, a confidence you will need when the going gets tough. Oh, by the way, the going nearly always gets tough in any leadership role!

In the scriptures, Joseph was clothed in the robes of Pharaoh in (Genesis 41:42), Joshua received the mantle of leadership from Moses (Deuteronomy 34:9), and Elisha received a double portion of Elijah's spiritual mantle to bring about prophetic leadership among the Hebrew people (1 Kings 19:19). A Mantle in the Old Testament was literally a shawl or scarf, worn by a previous leader, given to the next one. It was a symbol of authority and responsibility. As a Man of God, the mantle of leadership is figurative; it is a word that is symbolic of God's anointing or calling for you to take on the responsibility and authority for a work He wants you to carry out.

I've led Centerpoint Church for twenty years now. What was a struggling little church with around 50 people in worship in a storefront in a strip mall has become a large, flourishing, and impactful congregation. That dirt I sunk my hands into now is home to a fully built-out church campus with four buildings that facilitate a weekly attendance of nearly 3,000 people. The kid who didn't know what He was doing received a calling, a mantle for leadership. That mantle of leadership gave me spiritual strength to push and persevere, to keep going through countless struggles, pains, betrayals, losses, and problems. That is the value of leading from a place of calling!

Discern how God has given you a calling for your leadership assignment. Imagine Him placing a mantle around your shoulders as He says, "Son, I want you to do this work!" See yourself saying "Father, I accept your calling into this assignment and I receive Your mantle to do it!" Whether it is in your business, your department, your church ministry role, or your civic position, lead from knowing you have God's calling to do it, a mantle from your Heavenly Father to carry the burden of authority and responsibility with supernatural strength, dignity, and impact!

KINGS DISCUSSION QUESTIONS

1   What is your understanding of godly leadership? How would you define it?

Rate your leadership capacity (0 to 100) — if you were firing on all cylinders. Now rate your current leadership reality (0 to 100). Make a quick diagnosis: what's wrong?

2   **Read Proverbs 29:18, Jeremiah 29:11, and Habakkuk 2:1–3.** What is a vision or dream that God has given you for your life? How can you confidently pursue that vision, even in the face of obstacles or opposition? What problem does your vision solve? How will people feel when they get to that preferred future of your vision?

Share an area of life or business where you are not envisioning a better future and why you are neglecting this.

3   **Read Proverbs 16:1–9.** What are some practical steps you can take to achieve a specific goal or overcome a challenge in your life or business? How are you seeking God's guidance and direction as you establish your strategy?

Share about a way you have dropped the ball (in the past or currently) when it comes to creating a strategic plan and following up with thoughtful orchestration, and what the effect of that neglect was. Describe what you will do to correct that.

4   **Read Habakkuk 2:1–3 again and Proverbs 16:23.** How can you improve your communication skills in your personal relationships? In your workplace? In your community with the people you lead? How can you use your words to motivate and encourage people to join you in your cause?

Give an example of great communication in leadership that you've executed recently and describe what made it great.

5   **Read Ecclesiastes 4:9–11 again, 1 Thessalonians 5:11, and Romans 12:9–10.** What are some ways you can build trust and loyalty with the people around you, whether it's with your family, friends, or workers? What are you doing to inspire people around you to work together towards a common goal?

Do people in your orbit feel loved by you? Share about specific ways you have recently built trust and relationship with people who work for you or with you.

6   **Read Exodus 18:13–27 again and discuss.** How can you empower others to use their gifts and talents to achieve results as part of your team? What are some practical ways you can better develop people, and more strongly support and encourage them as they take action towards the vision?

How have you failed to delegate well in any recent leadership decisions?

ARISE AND ACCEPT THE CHALLENGE

1 Name a problem in your community and create a full leadership solution using the five steps above.

2 Write a list of ten people who work with you whom you need to build relationship and trust with. Immediately text or call them with some kind of encouragement.

3 Write a list of five problems in your company. Don't overthink; just write the first five that come to mind. Then, imagine a possible solution for each one. Imagine it and then write down the ideas for solutions. That's some fresh vision material!

Made in United States
Orlando, FL
05 April 2025

60168390R00085